Illustrator:
Howard Chaney

Editor:
Marsha Kearns

Editorial Project Manager:
Ina Massler Levin, M.A.

Editor in Chief:
Sharon Coan, M.S. Ed.

Art Director:
Elayne Roberts

Associate Designer:
Denise Bauer

Cover Artist:
Sue Fullam

Production Manager:
Phil Garcia

Imaging:
Alfred Lau
Ralph Olmedo, Jr.

Publishers:
Rachelle Cracchiolo, M.S. Ed.
Mary Dupuy Smith, M.S. Ed.

Interdisciplinary Unit
Ancient Greece
CHALLENGING

Author:

Michelle Breyer, M.A.

Teacher Created Materials, Inc.
P.O. Box 1040
Huntington Beach, CA 92647
ISBN-1-55734-575-9

©1996 Teacher Created Materials, Inc.   Made in U.S.A.

Table of Contents

Table of Contents *(cont.)*

Introduction

Ancient Greece is an exciting, whole language, interdisciplinary unit. Its pages are filled with a wide variety of lesson ideas, as well as reproducible pages, for use with intermediate and middle school students. The Ancient Greece theme is connected to the curriculum with individual, classroom, and cooperative learning activities in reading, language arts (written and oral), science, social studies, math, art, music, and life skills.

This unit is divided into the following sections to allow for easy thematic planning: Geography; Early Greek Cultures; Government; Economy, Trade, and Transportation; Religion; Society, Family, the Arts, and Education; Hellenistic Greece; Achievements; Living History—A Day in Ancient Greece; and Literature Connection. The lessons are designed so that they can be used in conjunction with social studies and science textbooks.

This interdisciplinary unit includes the following:

- **Bulletin Board and Transparency Ideas**—provide motivational, interactive, and informative ideas

- **Curriculum Connections**—incorporate skills in math, science, language arts, fine arts, and social studies

- **Visual and Performing Arts**—create opportunities for students in the areas of art, architecture, construction, drama, and music

- **Whole Language Experiences**—offer a wide variety of reading techniques, ideas for writing passages and poetry, and oral language activities

- **Group Projects and Activities**—foster cooperative learning strategies and critical thinking skills

- **Moments in Time**—transport students back in time through reading selections, readers theater, and reenactments

- **Living History**—A Day in Ancient Greece—provides research ideas, activities, and suggestions for re-creating a day in the life of the Ancient Greeks

- **Literature Connection**: *Adventures of the Greek Heroes*— a book and activities related to the theme

- **Technology**—suggests uses of technology that can be integrated throughout the unit and correlated with the theme

- **Bibliography**—lists additional materials related to the theme

Moments in Time—Readers Theater

Each section has an informative and fun read-aloud play or narrative about Ancient Greece. Through reenactment, students will experience "going back in time." Reproduce scripts for all the students so they can participate and/or read along as the plays or narratives are presented orally to the class. Use the scripts as springboards for introducing and discussing how the Ancient Greeks lived. Vocabulary and comprehension activities further students' understanding and knowledge of this important civilization.

4

Class Cluster

On the chalkboard or overhead, make a chart like the one below. Discuss as a class what you already know or believe about Ancient Greece. Record these items on the chart. On the other side of the chart record what aspects of our culture can be attributed to Ancient Greece. Items might include the following: democracy, architecture, certain words, geometry, medicine, and astronomy. Tell students that throughout the unit you will update the list of things attributed to the Greeks. If you wish, have students keep a list of their own in a notebook or social studies journal.

Things We Know About Ancient Greece	Things from Our Culture Attributed to the Ancient Greeks

Comparison Chart

Make a chart out of two pieces of tagboard to use throughout this unit and future units on ancient civilizations. Use a black marker and index cards to record information for each category. Tape the card onto the chart when studying that category. Use a different color of index card for each ancient civilization.

	Middle East	Egypt	Greece	Rome
Geography				
Economy				
Science				
Education and the Arts				
Religion				
Government				
Social Structure				

Vocabulary Journal

Staple lined paper into a construction paper cover or provide a composition book as a vocabulary journal for each student. As you work through the unit, have students record the section of study and the important vocabulary words for that section. Students should write a definition and illustration for each word. Allow students to do some of this as homework. Students can use their journals to study for the unit assessment. Tell students you may allow them to use their vocabulary journals during the unit assessment. This may motivate them to take accurate and thorough notes!

Motivational Videos

Motivate students by watching a video on Greek mythology. Check your local library and video stores for stories about the Greek gods or heroes. Remind students that movies may not accurately portray the story plot. Later in the unit when discussing mythological passages, you can refer to the videos and critique them.

Timeline Overview

After discussing what you already know about Ancient Greece, have students create a timeline to help them better understand the changes that occurred during the 2,000 years of Greek civilization.

Preparing for the lesson:

1. Make an overhead transparency of and reproduce for each student the Timeline Information (page 7).

2. Reproduce a Timeline Chart (pages 8 and 9) for each student.

3. Provide scissors, tape, and writing and coloring materials, such as crayons or colored pencils, for each student.

Teaching the lesson:

1. Distribute the Timeline Information and Timeline Chart. Have students cut apart the Timeline Chart and set the pieces alongside one another to form one long strip. Have students tape the pieces together without overlapping edges so it reads "Ancient Greece."

❖ A N C I E N T ~ G R E E C E ❖

2. Have students notice the time frames already written on the timeline. Note that the dates go backwards and elicit that is because they indicate B.C. time. If you have previously studied other ancient civilizations, compare their beginning and ending dates with those of Ancient Greece.

3. Display the Timeline Information overhead transparency to use as a guide, and discuss the major events that occurred in each period or age. Have students label each period or age on their timeline. Then have students write in the dates and information for each period.

❖ A N C I E N T ~ G R E E C E ❖

| | | Early Greek Cultures | | Dark Age | Archaic Period | Classical Age | Hellenistic Period | |

4. Once all information has been correctly recorded, have students color each period or age time span lightly with a different color. Remind students that they need to be able to read through the coloring. Have students note which periods or ages lasted a long time and which periods or ages were very short. Discuss possible reasons for this.

5. Have students decorate their timelines and choose some to display around the classroom or have students store them in a folder for use throughout the unit.

Timeline Information

Early Greek Cultures 2000–1100 B.C.

2000 The Minoans begin the Bronze Age and live in small farming and fishing communities. They flourish on the island of Crete and develop a writing system.

1900–1450 The Minoans build the Palace at Knossos and dominate the Aegean Sea.

1450 A volcanic eruption destroys the Minoan civilization. Crete is taken over by Mycenaeans.

1400 The Mycenaeans become the great power in Greece.

1280–1250 The Trojan War is fought by Mycenaean kings.

1200 Mycenaean power slowly declines.

The Dark Age 1100–800 B.C.

1100–800 The Dark Age results from the Dorian invasion of Greece from the north. There is little development of culture during this time.

The Archaic Period 800–470 B.C.

800 The Greeks develop poetry, sculpture, and pottery. Homer writes the *Iliad* and the *Odyssey*.

776 The first Olympic Games are held.

620 Written laws and punishments are documented.

570 The use of coins is introduced.

550–500 Sparta is founded and Athens establishes a democracy.

490–479 The Persian War is won by the Greeks and recorded by Herodotus, a great historian.

The Classical Age 470–336 B.C.

470 Socrates, a great philosopher, is born.

465–429 This is The Golden Age of Athens. Pericles brings Athens to the height of its power.

431–404 Sparta conquers Athens in the Peloponnesian War.

387 Plato, a student of Socrates, founds a philosophical school in Athens.

The Hellenistic Period 336–200 B.C.

336–330 Alexander the Great becomes king of Macedonia and unites many Greek states. He expands and conquers many lands, including Persia, Syria, Phoenicia, Egypt, and India.

323 Alexander dies in Babylon, and Greece is overrun by Macedonia.

200 Macedonia is defeated by the Romans, and Greece becomes part of the Roman Empire.

Timeline Chart

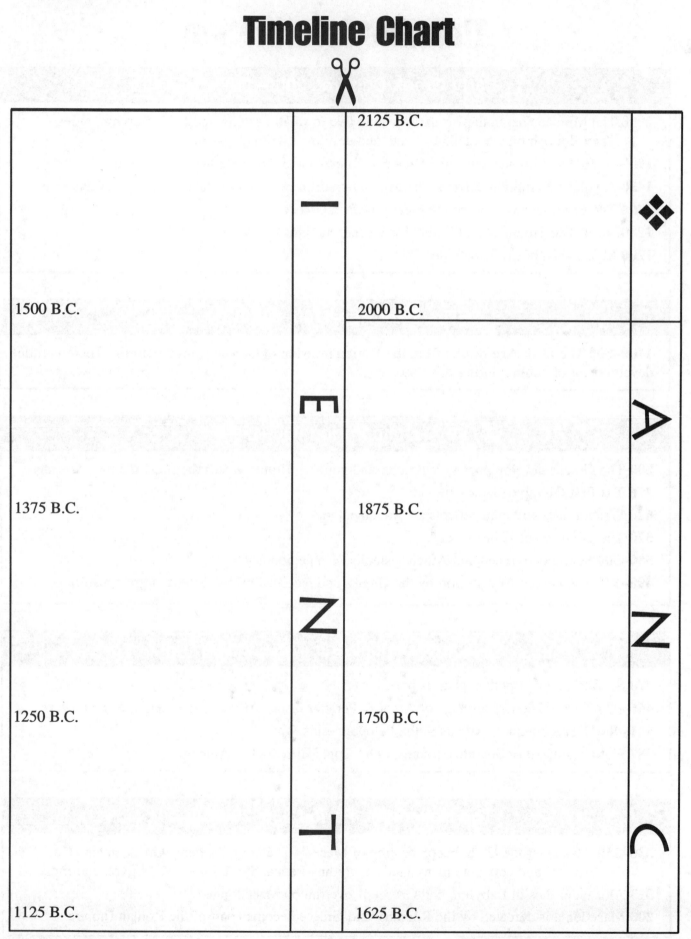

1500 B.C.

1375 B.C.

1250 B.C.

1125 B.C.

A N C I E N T

2125 B.C.

2000 B.C.

1875 B.C.

1750 B.C.

1625 B.C.

8

Timeline Chart *(cont.)*

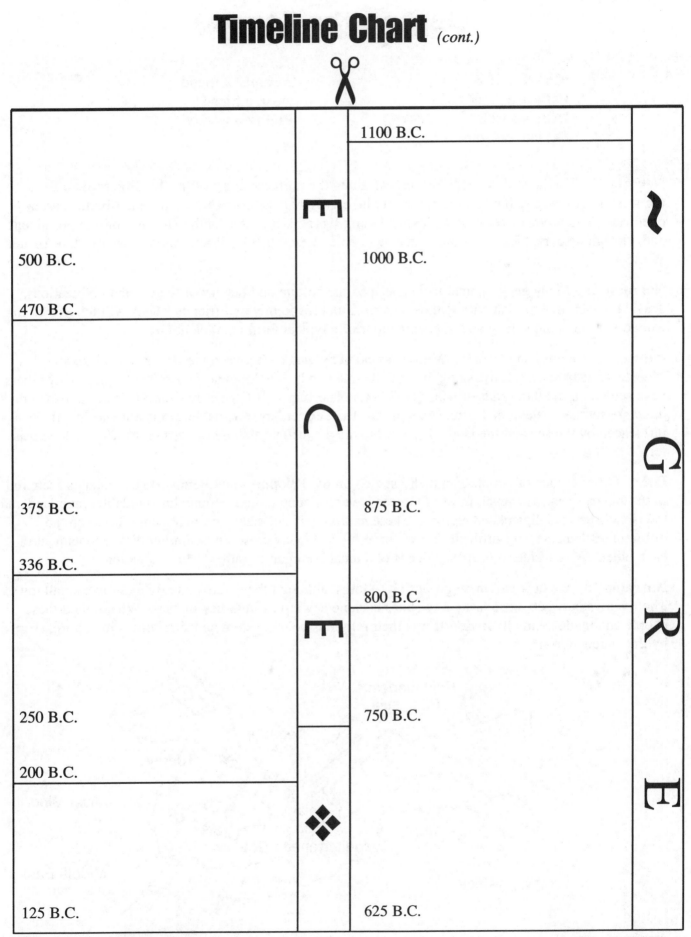

	GREECE
	1100 B.C.
500 B.C.	1000 B.C.
470 B.C.	
375 B.C.	875 B.C.
336 B.C.	
	800 B.C.
250 B.C.	750 B.C.
200 B.C.	
125 B.C.	625 B.C.

Pathos the Farmer

Narrators 1–5
Pathos, a farmer
Dela, his wife
Dorian, his son

Acropis, a friend
Zetu, a friend
Plutos, a worker

Narrator 1: The land of Ancient Greece lies along the northern coast of the **Mediterranean Sea**. To the west is present-day Italy and Europe. To the east is Asia Minor, Turkey, and the Middle Eastern countries. The northern coast of Africa, including Egypt, sits to the south. Because of this prominent and strategic geographical position, Greece was able to establish itself as a major power of the Ancient World.

Narrator 2: Many geographical factors shaped the culture and history of the ancient civilizations. Travel back in time to visit with Pathos, a farmer, and his family and friends. They will tell you of the wonders of this unique land and give you a tour of a typical farm in Ancient Greece.

Pathos: Welcome, my friends. We live bounded by water—between the **Aegean**, **Ionian**, and **Mediterranean seas**. Many people live on the mainland, or Peloponnesus Peninsula, and many others have settled on the thousands of islands offshore. The very first Greek civilization was established on the large southern island of **Crete**. As with most Greek settlements, its development was greatly influenced by the sea and the land. The sea provided excellent fishing opportunities and the land was fertile.

Dela: Other groups of people eventually settled on the **Peloponnesus Peninsula** and islands scattered in the Aegean Sea. However, most of Greece is very mountainous. Mountains divide the mainland and the islands into small, isolated regions. These natural barriers make communication between the different settlements very difficult. So we have formed many close-knit communities independent of each other. We consider ourselves citizens of a local community rather than of a nation.

Narrator 3: We now call these groups **city-states**, although they were actually more like small towns. The rivalries between these many city-states became key issues in Greek history. What united these people and made them all Greek? It was their religious belief system and similarities in culture, shaped by this unique terrain.

Pathos the Farmer *(cont.)*

Acropis: In addition to the mountains and islands, the sea has greatly influenced the development of our Greek civilization and culture. The sea has become our vital link between communities on the mainland and the islands. More and more people now travel by sea, allowing us to share ideas and trade. Mastering travel on the seas has allowed us to build a powerful navy and gain a common identity.

Narrator 4: The sea, the mountains, and the islands were also the source of many fears and tales of adventure. Because people were cut off from other communities, many wild tales would arise from travelers claiming to have visited lands with unusual creatures and powers. Eventually these tales became part of the Greek culture itself, and we enjoy them today as Greek mythology.

Zetu: As my friends have mentioned, Greece is a land of high mountains. These were once covered by trees, but as our population has grown we cleared them irresponsibly and allowed the good soil to wash away. This means we have a limited amount of space and land suitable for growing crops. This is very unfortunate, because our hot and sunny climate would allow crops to grow year-round. Our dry land cannot support large herds of animals, either, but we use oxen, mules, and donkeys to pull carts. We keep pigs and poultry to provide luxury foods at dinner parties. Our most common animal is the goat, which lives happily in our dry climate. They provide milk, meat, and skins. The very rich own land with lush plant life, so they are able to raise horses.

Dorian: Come now and visit our family farmlands. We grow our crops in the hill country that lies between the coastal plains and the mountains. Many farmers, like my father, build terraces on the slopes to increase their farmland. Here we grow grapes, olives, pears, apples, and pomegranates. Other important crops include peas and beans. Since flat, fertile land for growing grains is in short supply, we trade our products with other countries for these much needed grains. Wheat and barley are made into bread, porridge, and beer. My parents will accompany you to the next ridge, and you can watch Plutos as he plows the fields with our other workers.

Pathos the Farmer *(cont.)*

Plutos: My plow is made from the curved branch of a tree that is dragged through the soil by an ox. Behind me walks the sower, who scatters seeds in my footsteps. At harvest time we will cut the crops with a curved blade called a sickle. If you look beyond my field you can see Pathos' olive grove. Olive trees flourish in this dry, rocky soil. It is now harvest time for the olives. One man sits in the tree and shakes the branches while others below gather the fallen fruit in their baskets.

Pathos: Olives and grapes are our most prevalent and useful crops. The fruit of the olive can be eaten or crushed to make oil for cooking and for eating on bread. We also use olive oil with scented herbs to clean and moisturize our skin instead of soap. Olive oil is essential for use in our clay lamps, which provide the main form of light in our homes. We believe that the goddess Athena gave the gift of the olive tree to us Greeks by striking her spear into the rock of the Acropolis. From this spot grew the first olive tree.

Dela: Grapes also provide a good source of fruit. They are crushed to make juice or wine. Grape and olive products are easy to grow here and useful for trade with other countries, as is honey. Honey is the only sweetener used throughout the world we know. Beekeeping is widespread throughout Greece. Plato once said about the farmlands in Greece: "What now remains . . . is like the bones of a body wasted and diseased, with all the rich and fertile earth fallen away and only the scraggy skeleton of the land left and the mountains supporting nothing but bees."

Narrator 5: As you have learned, the unique geography of Greece was influential in shaping its economy, culture, and history. The Greeks' prowess on the sea allowed them to make contact with other people and countries. They evolved into a civilization influenced by others but remained distinctive in their beliefs and way of life.

12

Pathos the Farmer—
Vocabulary and Comprehension

The following words from the story can be used by students in their Vocabulary Journals (page 5). Remind students to write a complete definition of each word and illustrate them if they wish.

Mediterranean Sea	**Peloponnesus Peninsula**
Ionian Sea	**Crete**
Aegean Sea	**city-states**

All or some of the following questions can be used for whole class discussion, small group work, or individual assessment. Allow students to refer back to the passage while working.

1. How did the mountains and islands influence the development of individual city-states? *(They formed natural barriers that made it difficult for people to interact and form one large, unified country.)*

2. How is the location of Greece on the Mediterranean Sea beneficial for trade and expansion? *(Greece is located in the middle of the Mediterranean Sea, near many other flourishing civilizations. Water travel allowed them to reach many areas for trade and conquest.)*

3. In what ways did the sea shape Greek culture, myth, economy, and trade? *(The sea was a main feature in daily life. In order to survive, the Greeks were forced to learn new ways to travel upon the water. The sea was their main highway for trade with other lands and expansion into new territories. The voyages into new and unknown areas prompted the tales of mystical places and exaggerations now known as the Greek myths.)*

4. Why didn't the Ancient Greeks have large herds of animals or large quantities of grain? *(They did not have enough grazing land or flat fertile areas for growing large quantities of grain.)*

5. Describe a typical Ancient Greek farm. *(Created on a hillside with terraces, the farms would be plowed and sowed with crops that could withstand the dry climate and rocky soil.)*

6. Why are olives such an important crop? *(Olive trees grew easily in the climate and soil conditions and provide people many things, such as a fruit and oil for eating, making cosmetics, and light. Olives were also a good source for trading with other areas.)*

7. Look up the words "peninsula" and "archipelago" in a dictionary. Describe how each of these are important in the study of Greece. *(The entire Greek mainland is a peninsula. An archipelago is a chain of islands, which describes the rest of the Greek territory off the coast.)*

Make a Map

Use an atlas and the directions below to label the map of Ancient Greece.

1. Three seas have played an important role in the history of Greece. Label the following: Mediterranean Sea, Aegean Sea, Ionian Sea.

2. Label the following areas on the map: Persian Empire, Macedonia, Thessaly, Attica, Peloponnesus, Thrace.

3. Label the island of Crete and the city of Knossos, where Greek civilization began.

4. Label the following important city-states: Mycenae, Troy (Abydos).

5. The Greeks believed their gods lived atop their highest mountain. Label Mount Olympus.

6. Label the following: Athens, Sparta, Delphi, Argos.

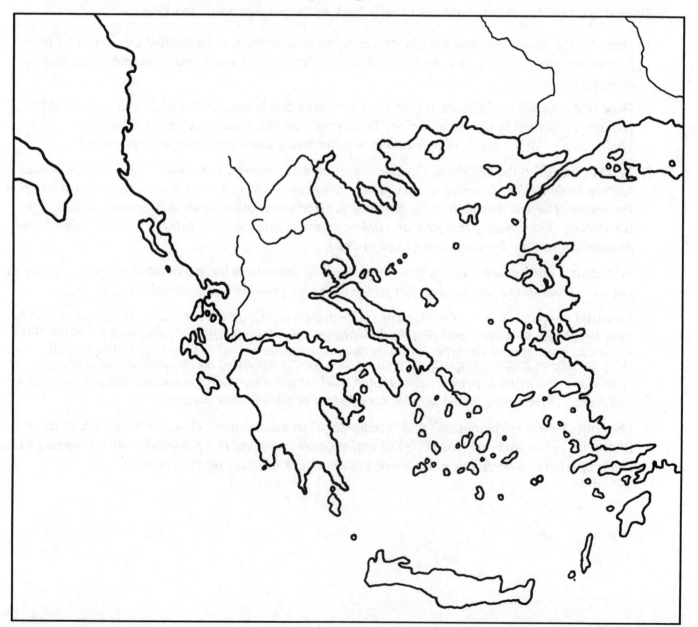

Geography Bulletin Board

Make an overhead transparency of the map on page 10. Use it to make a large map of Greece on a piece of tagboard. Have students gather pictures showing the geographic features of Greece from magazines and travel brochures. Place the tagboard map in the center of a bulletin board. Surround the map with pictures showing the different features of the land. Use yarn to connect the features to certain locations on the map. Throughout the unit, add pictures to your bulletin board that correspond to your section of study.

Describe a Mythical Land

Infrequent travel throughout the many small regions isolated by mountains and islands often resulted in misunderstanding and exaggeration. People interpreted unusual things they found in these remote areas in their own ways, making up stories and giving these things mythical qualities. For example, the tale of the Cyclops may have come from the discovery of elephant skulls. Such an enormous skull with a large hole in the center of the forehead (where the trunk had been) had never been seen. People assumed it was from a giant with one large eye, and they named it Cyclops. Have students create their own mythical lands with interesting creatures and write descriptive passages.

Preparing for the lesson:

1. Reproduce a Descriptive Writing Outline (page 16) and an Editing Checklist (page 18) for each student.

2. Make an overhead transparency of the Descriptive Writing Outline and The Writing Process (page 17).

3. Provide crayons, markers, or colored pencils for students to illustrate their compositions.

4. Gather short stories describing the different creatures and lands in Greek Mythology, and provide dictionaries and thesauruses for students' use.

Teaching the lesson:

1. Discuss the geography of Greece and its influence on Greek mythology. Read aloud some short stories as examples of the types of lands and creatures described in Greek mythology. Tell students that they will each write a descriptive passage describing a mythical place in Greece.

2. Display the transparency of The Writing Process and review it with the class.

3. Distribute the Descriptive Writing Outlines and tell students they will use them for their prewriting stage. Use the transparency to review the different parts of a descriptive passage. Remind students that they are not writing a story, but describing a mythological land and its inhabitants.

4. Allow students to use the dictionaries and thesauruses to elaborate on their descriptions.

5. When students have completed their prewriting and first drafts, distribute the Editing Checklists and describe how students should use them to enhance their compositions with the help of peer editors.

6. Have students illustrate their final drafts and display them in the room.

Descriptive Writing Outline

I. Introduction: (Get the reader hooked with some interesting background.)

_____

_____

_____

II. Body:

 Sights: _____

_____

_____

 Sounds: _____

_____

_____

 Smells: _____

_____

_____

 Textures/Touch: _____

_____

 Feelings: _____

_____

III. Conclusion: (Leave the reader with something to think about.)

_____

_____

_____

The Writing Process

PREWRITING

Cluster, outline, brainstorm, draw, and discuss your ideas.
Then make a plan to organize your ideas.

WRITING A FIRST DRAFT

Write down your ideas. Skip every other line. Use the information you recorded on your prewriting plan to organize your ideas in a logical manner. Do not worry about spelling, capitalization, punctuation, or grammar. Read over your first draft to be sure it makes sense.

GETTING A RESPONSE

Read your composition to a partner and get feedback to help clarify ideas. Have your partner help you identify the strengths and improve the weaknesses in your composition.

REVISING

Add details and descriptive words or phrases to your composition. You may need to change the sequence of sentences in order to clarify the ideas.

EDITING AND REWRITING

Have a second partner read your composition and help you make any grammatical and mechanical (spelling, capitalization, punctuation) corrections.

EVALUATING

Have your partners use the Editing Checklist to evaluate your composition.

PUBLISHING

Type or use your best handwriting to recopy your writing. Check it over again before turning it in to your teacher.

Editing Checklist

Name _____

Title _____

X = No changes needed   ✔ = Just okay   ✱ = Problem. Editor will help make corrections.

	1st Editor *listen and revise*	2nd Editor *read and revise*	Teacher's Comments
Proper format? (introduction, supporting details, conclusion)			
Specific supporting details? (use of metaphor, figurative language, similes, descriptions, examples, adjectives, adverbs, prepositional phrases, etc.)			
Correct sentence structure, grammar, and word use?			
Correct spelling?	✗		
Correct punctuation? (periods, commas, quotation marks)	✗		
Correct capitalization? (proper nouns, sentence beginnings)	✗		
Strengths of composition?			
Weaknesses of composition? (editors help make corrections)			

_____   _____

1st Editor   2nd Editor

The Minoans

The earliest Greek settlers arrived on the island of Crete around 6000 B.C. They most likely came by boat from Asia Minor. For thousands of years they lived peacefully in caves and simple huts, isolated from the rest of the world. Gradually they developed more sophisticated skills, until they grew to be a major power in the area.

Archaeologists have estimated the population to have reached nearly 100,000 during the height of Minoan Civilization, between 2000 B.C. and 1450 B.C. Sometime after 2000 B.C. the Minoans built a grand palace at Knossos. The palace itself covered at least six acres and was a complicated arrangement of rooms and chambers that twisted and turned. It even had a plumbing system with indoor toilets! The interior of the palace was decorated with large colored paintings showing how the Minoans worked and played.

Two major factors contributed to the growth and prosperity of the Minoan civilization. One was the sea; the other was the land. The calm waters of the Mediterranean Sea that surround the island proved to be excellent fishing grounds. The Minoans also constructed a large naval and merchant fleet of ships. These boats were built for long voyages, powered by sails and oars. The Minoans traded their wares as far off as Syria and Egypt.

The Minoans proved to be excellent farmers, and Crete is blessed with a vast amount of fertile soil. At the palace of Knossos, archaeologists have discovered large jars of olive oil, grains, honey, and other food crops. The Minoans were able to grow more food than the local population could consume, and they had an abundance of other resources, such as timber and wool. Their prosperity grew through exporting their surplus goods.

Their trading abilities and wealth allowed the Minoans to import materials they did not have locally. From imported gold, silver, other metals, and fabrics, Minoan craftsman created delicate jewelry, elaborate clothing, and ornaments. Minoan paintings show that women wore long, patterned, and intricately embroidered gowns with many layers of petticoats. Men and women alike wore jewelry.

Minoan potters were regarded as the best in the world, and their wares were much sought after throughout the Mediterranean region. Their distinctive pottery used a technique known as "sgraffito" to etch designs and figures onto their pottery. (What word does "sgraffito" remind you of? How is the modern-day "graffiti" similar in technique to the ancient "sgraffito"?) Many Grecian urns showed mythological tales, glimpses of everyday farming life, or intricate patterns and symbols indicative of a certain region.

The Minoans *(cont.)*

Archaeologists have discovered that the Minoans were a fascinating people. They appear to have enjoyed many sports, including boxing and a dangerous form of acrobatics performed with bulls. Young men and women competed in teams. The members would grasp a bull's horns and use them to flip over the bull and into the arms of a teammate. This bull-leaping was probably similar to a modern-day rodeo.

Women were accorded special status because they were responsible for bearing the children who assured the continued existence of the Minoan civilization. Some historians believe this high regard for women stemmed from the Minoan main deity—the Mother Goddess, or Snake Goddess. Snakes were worshipped in every household as guardians of the home, and only those women blessed by the Mother Goddess were permitted to bear children. The queens of Knossos may have even been worshipped as representatives of the Mother Goddess herself. Because of this elevated status, Minoan women appear to have enjoyed many freedoms that were denied women in other ancient cultures. They participated in sports, hunted, and attended sports and other cultural events, such as the theater.

Around 1450 B.C. the Minoan civilization began to decline. On Thera, an island north of Crete, a huge volcanic explosion killed all inhabitants of Thera and created a massive cloud of volcanic ash that engulfed Crete. Most of the eastern and northern parts of the island were covered in thick layers of ash that destroyed the land and made it useless for farming.

Then part of the island of Thera collapsed, creating earthquakes and spawning tidal waves over 500 feet high. Huge walls of water crashed upon the shores of Crete, devastating the Minoan ship fleets. Clouds of choking ash darkened the skies and suffocated animals and people. Fires swept through buildings ignited by flying ash, and poisonous fumes and gases drifted across the island. The capital, Knossos, was spared the worst damage because it was located inland.

These natural disasters probably made the Minoans believe they were being punished and destroyed by their gods. Physically and morally weakened, they were now easy prey for invaders from the north, mainly Mycenaean Greeks—a rough and crude people who eventually overthrew the government at Knossos and destroyed the palace. Still, the Minoan culture endured for many more centuries. The influences of Minoan farming, religion, art, and architecture greatly influenced the new Mycenaean civilization and helped Greece again achieve great power in the Mediterranean region.

20

Minoan Facts

Answer the following questions in complete sentences.

1. What were some of the achievements of the Minoans? _____

   _____

   _____

2. How did the treatment of Minoan women differ from other ancient civilizations? _____

   _____

   _____

3. What eventually destroyed the Minoan civilization? _____

   _____

   _____

Message from Knossos

Pretend that you are a citizen of Knossos at the time of the natural disasters on Crete. Write a diary entry below describing who you are, what you do, and how you feel about the volcano, earthquakes, and tidal waves that are destroying your civilization. (Use the back of this page as needed.)

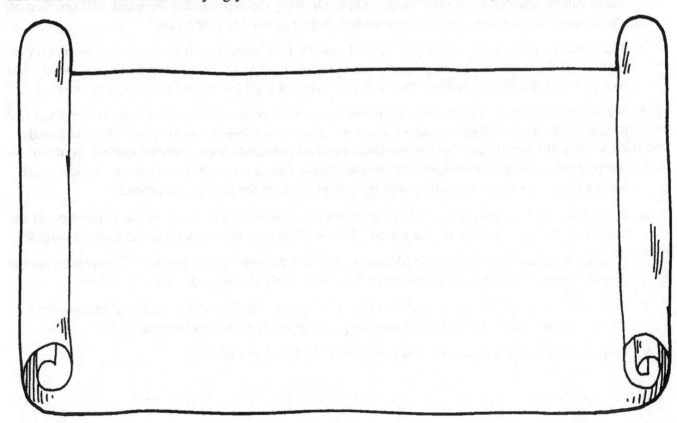

Minoan Pottery

The Minoans were famous worldwide for their pottery. Have students use the etching technique known as *sgraffito* to create elaborate Grecian urns.

Preparing for the lesson:

1. Gather for each student two 9" x 12" (23 cm x 30 cm) sheets of orange construction paper, thick red and orange crayons, black tempera paint, a paintbrush, a piece of scratch paper 8½" x 11" (22 cm x 28 cm), and an etching implement such as a mechanical pencil or large bent paper clip.

2. Cover all work areas with butcher paper or plastic to protect from paint and etchings.

3. Reproduce a copy of Minoan Pottery Styles (pages 23 and 24) for each student.

4. Make a sample urn before teaching the lesson so you can better help students.

Teaching the lesson:

1. Show students your sample and distribute the copies of Minoan Pottery Styles. Discuss the different types of pottery, noting the intricate patterns and the figures and scenes depicted.

2. Tell students that they are going to create their own Minoan pottery using the "sgraffito" etching technique. Have them choose a pottery shape and appropriate scene.

3. Distribute one sheet of orange construction paper and crayons to each student. Have students prepare their paper by HEAVILY coloring the paper with crayon. It is best if students work on one area of the paper until it is completely and heavily coated then move on to another area. There can be absolutely no construction paper showing through or else the paint will not etch off. The orange and red crayon represents the red clay they used to make pots.

4. Then have students paint on a layer of black paint. This represents the blackening of the clay as it is fired. If the paper is coated properly with crayon, the paint will resist and not coat evenly and easily. Once this first coat dries, they can paint over it until the paper is completely covered.

5. While waiting for the paint to dry, distribute the scratch paper and have students sketch their Grecian urn. Tell students to make the urn as large as possible to fill the page. This will make drawing in the details and figures much easier. Have students use different features from the samples given or design features of their own in the Greek style. Tell students to decide which parts will remain black and which will be etched to show the orange underneath.

6. Once the paint is completely dry, have students place their sketch on top of the painted paper and trace over the lines heavily with a pencil. This will transfer their design to the painted surface.

7. Have students use their etching implements to create their design on the urn. This represents the potters etching away the blackened surface of the pottery to reveal the red clay below.

8. Have students carefully cut around the edge of their urn, leaving a thin border of black paint. Then have them glue their urn onto another piece of orange construction paper.

9. Display the urns on a bulletin board covered in black butcher paper.

Minoan Pottery Styles

Practical in design, Minoan pottery was painted with a wide variety of subjects, including religious, mythological, and scenes from everyday life. Heroes from Greek mythology, such as Hercules, Theseus and the Minotaur, and Apollo, were common subjects, as were Olympic athletes, musicians, chariots, and farming.

Water was collected from the public fountains in a jar called a *hydria*. It had three handles— one at the top and one on each side.

Greek women liked to use scented oils. Small containers called *lekthos* were used to hold different types.

Water, wine, olive oil, or grains were stored in two-handled containers called *amphoras*.

Minoan Pottery Styles *(cont.)*

Wine and water were poured from jars called *oinochoes*. These each had one handle and a spout.

These liquids would then be poured into long, flat, two-handled drinking cups called *kylix*.

The extremely sweet Minoan wine was diluted with water at the table. Wine and water were mixed in a large, two-handled bowl called a *krater*.

Theseus and the Minotaur

Long ago the island of Crete was ruled by a powerful leader named King Minos. Legend claims he was the son of Zeus and Europa and therefore was looked upon favorably by the gods on Mount Olympus. His beautiful wife was daughter of Helios, the sun god. King Minos loved his wife and built her an elaborate palace at Knossos. He called upon his clever architect to perfect the design of spiraling staircases and twisting corridors. The palace was filled with beautiful paintings worshipping the bull-god, a tribute to Zeus, who, in the shape of a bull, had brought the queen to the island.

The royal couple lived in peace and prosperity for many years. However, Poseidon, the god of the sea, soon grew jealous of his brother Zeus. He felt the people of Crete should worship him since it was his watery kingdom that surrounded their island. One day he sent a snowy-white bull to Crete. He demanded that the bull be sacrificed in his honor. But the queen grew fond of the bull and pleaded with her husband to spare its life. King Minos could not deny his beautiful wife, and the bull was spared. Enraged by the king's defiance, Poseidon used his magic to make the bull go mad. It ravaged the island, and soon all appeared to be doomed.

As chance would have it, Hercules caught wind of King Minos' plight. He sailed to Crete and took the mad bull away. The kingdom rejoiced and the people began restoring their island. But Poseidon was still angry. To further punish the disobedient king and queen, he made the queen bear a hideous child—half bull and half man. This monster was called the Minotaur, and it ate only human flesh. The king once again went to his clever architect and had him construct an elaborate labyrinth under the palace to house the beast.

As long as the Minotaur was given victims to eat, the palace was peaceful. When the Minotaur grew hungry, his blood-curdling bellows sent shivers down the spines of everyone throughout the kingdom. King Minos was forced to wage war against neighboring regions in order to supply the Minotaur with food. During a battle in Athens, King Minos' son was killed. As revenge, he demanded King Aegeus, the king of Athens, to send 14 young Athenian men and women to Crete to be sacrificed to the Minotaur. Minos told King Aegeus that a boat with black sails would come every nine years to transport the youths to Crete. If King Aegeus did not comply, Minos threatened to destroy Athens.

Theseus and the Minotaur *(cont.)*

King Aegeus was distraught, but he knew King Minos' armies were more powerful than his own, so he complied. For more than 20 years the black-sailed ships came and carried away the doomed. Then one day, word came to Athens that a young hero named Theseus was traveling throughout Greece overpowering evil. When King Aegeus heard the news he was overjoyed, for this young hero was none other than his own son. At the time of his secret birth, King Aegeus had buried a sword and golden sandals under a boulder. He told Theseus's mother, "When Theseus is clever and strong enough to lift the boulder, he may bring these things to Athens and claim the throne as my rightful heir."

When Theseus arrived in Athens, he presented his father with the sword and golden sandals. King Aegeus was proud to see that his son had grown into a strong and handsome man with a good heart. That same day the ship with black sails returned, and Athens mourned the 14 young men and women chosen for this dreadful voyage. Seeing his father's pain, Theseus begged to go to Crete and destroy the Minotaur once and for all. King Aegeus was reluctant, but finally gave in and Theseus joined the group. Before leaving, Theseus told the king, "Do not worry, dear father. The gods are with me, so I can only succeed in my mission. I promise that once again Athens will be free. As a sign of my victory, I will hoist white sails when we return." With that, Theseus sailed away with the others to Crete. Once on the island of Crete, Theseus and the other prisoners were taken to the palace, where they bathed and attended a grand banquet. The doomed Athenians were so frightened they could not eat. Only Theseus, filled with confidence, ate and drank heartily. The king's daughter, Ariadne, was taken by this bold behavior and spent the evening talking and laughing with Theseus. By the end of the evening, she was madly in love with him. As the prisoners were taken to the dungeon to sleep, Ariadne knew she must save Theseus or die heartbroken.

That night she secretly stole away to the architect's chambers and begged him to save her one true love. The architect finally gave in, handling Ariadne a magic ball of golden thread. He instructed her to take Theseus to the gates of the labyrinth at midnight while the Minotaur slept. Theseus was to place the ball of gold thread on the ground and then follow it through the maze as it magically unwound through the twisting corridors. However, he had no magic to help Theseus once he met the Minotaur. Theseus was on his own.

Ariadne thanked the architect and sneaked off to meet Theseus. She confessed her undying love and offered to help him if only he would take her away and make her his wife. Theseus kissed Ariadne and gladly agreed. They quietly crept to the large gates of the labyrinth. There they tied the end of the thread to a post.

26

Theseus and the Minotaur *(cont.)*

Ariadne wished Theseus good luck and waited in anticipation as he followed the gold ball into the darkness. He twisted and turned throughout the dizzying maze, keeping one step behind the speeding ball. Soon he heard the loud snore of the Minotaur and smelled the sour stench of death. Around the bend he emerged into a room filled with bleached bones and skulls. In the middle slept the dreaded giant Minotaur. At once the beast awoke and charged at his intruder, surprised to find this midnight snack.

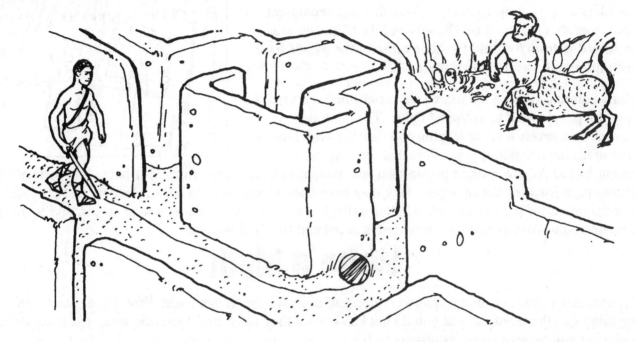

The Minotaur had not anticipated the strength of Theseus. For years most victims had fainted at the mere sight of the dreadful monster, allowing him to devour his meal without a fight. But Theseus appeared not only undaunted, but determined to put forth a brave struggle. Soon they were locked in a tangle of arms and horns. Loud bellowing grunts filled the dark chamber, until finally one last wheezing snort left the monster's snout as his bull-head hit the floor. Theseus had killed the Minotaur with his bare hands. Quickly, Theseus followed the golden thread back to the entrance. He freed the other victims and they all, including Ariadne, sprinted back to the ship. In his haste to leave, he forgot to change to white sails.

Theseus was filled with joy! No more Athenians would be sacrificed to the Minotaur, and he was returning home with a beautiful bride. That night he expected to sleep in peace. But the god of wine, Dionysus, appeared in his dreams. He told Theseus that this marriage was forbidden and that Ariadne could not be his wife. He told Theseus to leave Ariadne on the island of Naxos, where she must complete her destiny. Sadly, Theseus complied. As he sailed away broken-hearted, Dionysus appeared to Ariadne and made her his own wife. They lived happily together.

Theseus sailed on to Athens, still not having changed the black sails. As the ship entered the harbor, King Aegeus saw the black sails. Unable to bear the thought that he had sent his own son to his death, the old king flung himself off the cliff into the churning sea and rocks below. Theseus arrived to find his father dead and the kingdom his own. He vowed to rule and protect Athens from any future harm. So that his father would never be forgotten, he named the sea in his honor. To this day Athens stands as a pinnacle of strength with the waters of the Aegean Sea protecting its shores.

Was the Minotaur Real?

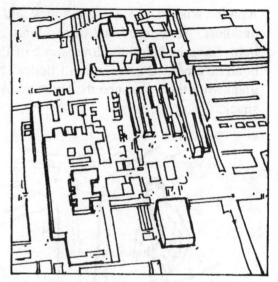

At the beginning of the 20th century, an Englishman named Arthur Evans organized an excavation of the site at Knossos. Arthur and his colleagues found the ruins of a palace that had been destroyed hundreds of years prior to the age of Classical Greece. The palace was an example of skillful architecture with an unusual design of complex twisting corridors and winding chambers. Was this archaeological find proof that the myth of Theseus and the Minotaur was grounded in truth? Could the huge maze of the palace have been interpreted as the labyrinth itself?

Many paintings within the palace also confirmed the myth's tale of a people who worshipped bulls. The paintings showed dangerous feats of leaping and dancing with bulls. Historians believe that it is possible that the king of this region forced Athens to send young men and women to Crete in the form of tribute. But instead of becoming a feast for the Minotaur, they may have been forced to train as bull-leapers and provide entertainment for the royal court. Undoubtedly, the leapers did not enjoy a long career, and word may have spread to Athens that they were being sacrificed to a bull monster.

Write a Myth

Pretend that you are in an unexplored region and discover the things listed. You have never seen anything like them before, and you do not know what they truly are. Describe what you have found and what you believe it and its powers to be.

1. The skeleton of a giraffe _____

   _____

2. Airplanes flying through the sky _____

   _____

3. A bubbling hot spring with animal tracks around it _____

   _____

4. A giant stone sculpture showing the head of a man and the body of a lion _____

   _____

5. A swarm of bats coming out of cave_____

   _____

6. Snowshoe tracks in newly fallen snow _____

   _____

Make a Kaleidoscope Labyrinth

After reading "Theseus and the Minotaur," have students use their geometry skills to design a kaleidoscope labyrinth of their own.

Preparing for the lesson:

1. Gather a variety of brightly colored 12" x 12" (30 cm x 30 cm) construction paper.

2. Provide each student with a compass, ruler, thin black marker, pencil, and scissors.

3. Make a sample prior to teaching the lesson.

Teaching the lesson:

1. Remind students that the palace at Knossos had intricately patterned corridors and twisting chambers that appeared to be like a labyrinth or maze. Tell students that they are going to create labyrinth-type pictures using repeating patterns.

2. Have each student select a piece of colored construction paper and distribute the other drawing materials.

3. Show students how to find the center of a paper by folding it into fourths but NOT creasing it except at the center point.

4. Have students begin their labyrinth by lightly drawing a large circle on their paper using the compass and pencil. The circle should fill the entire page. Then have them lightly draw four to six smaller circles within the outer circle to create the labyrinth.

5. Have students use the ruler and pencil to divide the circle into four equal segments. Tell students that the designs they create should be identical in all four segments of the labyrinth.

6. Once their design is complete, have students use the black marker to trace over their designs and fill in spaces. Again, make sure all four segments are the same.

7. Have students cut out their completed labyrinths, and display them on a bulletin board. For more contrast, mount the designs on a contrasting piece of construction paper.

The Mycenaeans

On the mainland of Greece, in an area known as the Peloponnesus Peninsula, a group of people called the Mycenaeans were growing ever stronger. These people were developing culture and expanding at the very time that the Minoans were becoming weaker. The Mycenaeans had learned much from trading with the Minoans. They built their palaces in the Minoan style of architecture and adopted their form of writing. They had also built a strong fleet of ships able to capture trade routes and help them establish flourishing colonies. The Mycenaeans invaded and conquered Crete in 1450 B.C. and soon became the dominant civilization in the Aegean Sea region.

These people were named after Mycenae, the city they came from which sat high on a hill overlooking the vast plains of Argos. Unlike the Minoans, who had ample farmlands and fishing, living in this hilly region meant few natural resources, so the Mycenaeans became traders. Their position on the mainland enabled them to became distributors of products from other countries. The Mycenaeans were also fine craftsmen of weapons, jewelry, and other artifacts made from imported raw materials. They were especially famous for their bronze work. Bronze is a metal made from smelting copper and tin together.

The Mycenaeans were much more warlike than the Minoans. Their lack of resources and need to acquire goods from other lands may have led them to a life of invasion and conquest. It is possible that their warlike nature caused fighting amongst their own colonies and perhaps even the collapse of their own civilization. By 1150 B.C. the Mycenaean culture was weak and left them a prime target for the Dorians to invade from the north.

All of the Mycenaean cities fell to Dorian rule except for Athens. Historians believe its salvation was a secret underground supply of water in the Acropolis. When a city was under siege, the invaders would cut off its supply of water, and the people could not survive. Athens was able to maintain its culture as a haven and refuge for many others while isolated from the rest of the world during the Dorian rule.

The Dorians were uncivilized people possessing none of the skills and craftsmanship of the Minoans or the Mycenaeans. They were farmers rather than traders, so trade during their rule came to a standstill. The Dorians had no written language. Since most Mycenaeans had fled the area, soon all written language disappeared. Greece entered a period of decline called the Dark Age, which lasted from about 1100 B.C. to 800 B.C.

The Mycenaeans *(cont.)*

The oral tradition of the Greeks allowed much of the history and heritage to be passed down from one generation to another. Tales of the Mycenaean period were kept alive through songs and stories that were repeated during religious festivals or feasts. Around 800 B.C. many people from the Ionia region in central Greece built cities and ports to expand trade once again. These people had migrated from Athens, which had survived the Dorian attacks. A new written language soon developed based on the Ionic dialect and the Phoenician alphabet. It was from this region that the first works of Greek literature came. The famous poet Homer wrote stories and epic poems based on the songs and tales about the Mycenaeans.

For the Greeks, Homer was the ultimate symbol of poetry and eloquence. According to Greek tradition, Homer was a blind bard, a wandering storyteller with an unmatched ability to dramatize a narrative. He wrote two epic poems, or long poetic tales, that celebrated the battle deeds and travels of heroes and the influence of the gods. the *Iliad* recounts the story of the Mycenaeans during the Trojan War. Historians are still unsure whether the war actually occurred, but excavations in present-day Turkey have uncovered the remains of a city believed to be Troy. Furthermore, investigation indicates that a siege may have occurred during the Mycenaean period, so many believe that Homer's tale was based on fact. Homer's second tale, the *Odyssey*, describes Odysseus's perilous journey home from the Trojan War and his amazing encounters in foreign lands.

This new development in writing and culture marked the end of the Dark Age and the dawn of a new age of expansion called the Archaic Period.

Mycenaean Mysteries

Answer the following questions in complete sentences.

1. What were some contributions of the Mycenaeans to Greek culture? _____

   _____

2. How were the Mycenaeans different from the Minoans? _____

   _____

3. What happened to the Mycenaean civilization? _____

   _____

4. What was the Dark Age? _____

   _____

5. How did culture and trade return to Greece? _____

   _____

The Greek Alphabet

Based on the Phoenician alphabet, the Ionians developed a new written language containing 24 symbols. This alphabet contained letters for both consonants and vowel sounds, which was an improvement over the consonant-only version used by the Phoenicians. Use the chart below to write in Ancient Greek.

Small Case	Capital	Name	Modern
α	A	alpha	a
β	B	beta	b
γ	E	gamma	c, g
δ	X	delta	d
ε	Δ	epsilon	e
ζ	Z	zeta	z
η	H	eta	h, e
θ	Θ	theta	th
ι	I	iota	j, i
κ	K	kappa	k
λ	Λ	lambda	l
μ	M	mu	m
ν	N	nu	n
ξ	Ξ	xi	x
o	O	omicron	o
π	Π	pi	p
ρ	P	rho	r
σ	Σ	sigma	s
τ	T	tau	t
υ	Y	upsilon	u, y, w
φ	Φ	phi	f, ph, q
χ	X	chi	ch
ψ	Ψ	psi	ps
ω	Ω	omega	o

Using Ancient Greek

Nameplate with Motto

Have each student fold a piece of construction paper in half to form a long rectangle. On one half of the page, have students write their names and a motto or philosophical phrase that describes their outlooks on life. Have them use the chart on page 32 to write their names and mottos using Greek letters on the other half of the paper. Have students set their nameplates on their desks during the unit.

Greek Letters

Divide the class into pairs. Have each student use Greek letters to write a message to his/her partner. Have them trade papers, read the messages, and write the English versions. Have them check each other's translations for accuracy.

Greek Word Discovery

Provide dictionaries and encyclopedias for students. On the chalkboard, write the following list of word parts. Tell students that one out of every eight words we use today has a Greek origin. Have them look up the meanings of the word parts and find three other common words we use in English that incorporate the Greek word parts.

anthropos—human being
aristos—best
auto—self
bios—life
cracy—rule
demos—people
geo—earth

graphy—writing
homo—same
logy—study/science of
monos—one
philos—loving
phobia—fear
sophia—wisdom

The Mycenaean and Trojan War

The Trojan War from the Mycenaean Period is part of Homer's epic tales. The *Iliad* in its complete form is a long and imposing story. If you break its plot into sections and retell the events, students can gain an overview of the Trojan War and experience one of the most important pieces of Greek literature.

Preparing for the lesson:

1. Divide the class into eight groups, and reproduce the eight sections of the *Iliad* (pages 36–43) so that each person in the group has a copy of his/her section.

2. Create an overhead transparency of the *Iliad* Character Chart (page 35).

Teaching the lesson:

1. Tell students that they are going to learn about the Trojan War by studying Homer's account in the *Iliad.* Rather than read this huge piece of literature, they will work in groups to retell one section of the story. As a class they will put all of the sections in sequence to get a broad picture of the Trojan War.

2. Display the *Iliad* Character Chart and review each of the characters in the story. Then read aloud the following overview information to the class:

   The Trojan War was fought between the Mycenaean Greeks and the Trojans of Troy, a city located on the coast of Turkey. These two civilizations were very different. The Trojan people were linked to the Orient, where the main power belonged to the priests and monarchs. The Trojans believed that they were completely dependent upon the gods for their strength in battle and therefore continually sought divine guidance.

   On the other hand, the Greeks believed that they were in charge of their own destiny. They did acknowledge the important role the gods played in their daily lives. But they were much more individualistic and did not believe that they were completely dependent on the gods for the outcome of certain events.

   The Greek people treasured stories such as the *Iliad* as more than just a retelling of history. These stories helped to confirm their belief in the differences between themselves and the people in the Orient. And in a sense, the tales of Homer and others also gave them the hope and courage to persevere.

3. Tell the groups that they will each present their section of the *Iliad* to the class. They may use a narrator and have others in the group act out the parts, make large posters showing the action and read the information, make puppets to help retell the story, or choose another means of clearly presenting their part of this great epic. Assign a presentation due date, and allow class time for groups to prepare.

4. Display the overhead of the *Iliad* Character Chart as each group tells its part of the story. On the chalkboard make a note of key elements (conflict, role of gods, magic, royalty, heroic qualities, etc.) Allow students to copy and use these notes to complete all or some of the other activities in this lesson.

Iliad Character Chart

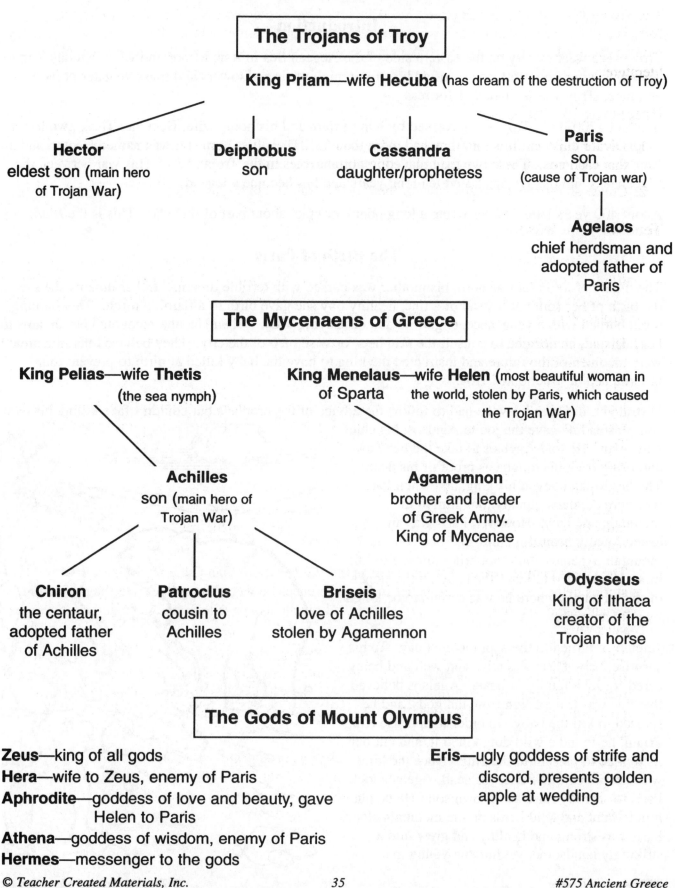

The Trojans of Troy

King Priam—wife **Hecuba** (has dream of the destruction of Troy)

Hector
eldest son (main hero
of Trojan War)

Deiphobus
son

Cassandra
daughter/prophetess

Paris
son
(cause of Trojan war)

Agelaos
chief herdsman and
adopted father of
Paris

The Mycenaens of Greece

King Pelias—wife **Thetis**
(the sea nymph)

King Menelaus—wife **Helen** (most beautiful woman in
of Sparta   the world, stolen by Paris, which caused
the Trojan War)

Achilles
son (main hero of
Trojan War)

Agamemnon
brother and leader
of Greek Army.
King of Mycenae

Chiron
the centaur,
adopted father
of Achilles

Patroclus
cousin to
Achilles

Briseis
love of Achilles
stolen by Agamennon

Odysseus
King of Ithaca
creator of the
Trojan horse

The Gods of Mount Olympus

Zeus—king of all gods
Hera—wife to Zeus, enemy of Paris
Aphrodite—goddess of love and beauty, gave
Helen to Paris
Athena—goddess of wisdom, enemy of Paris
Hermes—messenger to the gods

Eris—ugly goddess of strife and
discord, presents golden
apple at wedding

The *Iliad*—Section 1

Introduction

Troy was a wealthy city on the eastern side of the Aegean Sea in Asia Minor and what is today Turkey. Troy was large, beautiful, and fortified by strong, high walls and towers and massive gates at its entrance. Troy was a citadel, or fortress.

In about 1200 B.C., Troy was governed by King Priam and his noble wife, Hecuba. These two had a fondness for children; it is said they had more than 50! Their first-born son was named Hector, and a later son was Paris. These two men played important roles in the Trojan War. This war between the Mycenaens and the Trojans lasted ten long years and has become a legend.

About 400 years later, Homer wrote a long poem, or epic, about part of this war. This is the *Iliad*.

The Birth of Paris

The night before Paris was born, his mother was cursed with terrible dreams. In her dreams she saw the birth of her son, but instead of a fine, healthy boy she gave birth to a flaming torch. This flaming torch burned with a vengeance, engulfing and destroying Troy. When Hecuba recounted her dreams to her husband, he decided to consult the prophets, or wise men of the city. They believed that the dreams were an omen of the future and instructed the king to have the baby killed at birth to prevent this preordained destruction of Troy.

Distraught, the king knew he had to follow the advice of the prophets but couldn't face killing his own son. Instead he gave the job to Agelaos, his chief herdsman. He told Agelaos to take the baby away and bring back his tongue as proof of his death. The herdsman obeyed his king, and when Paris was born Agelaos quickly took him to the mountains of Troy. However, Paris was an exceptionally beautiful child, and once on the mountain Agelaos could not bring himself to kill him. He decided to leave the baby on the slopes of the mountain where he was certain to be killed by wild animals.

Agelaos returned to the spot the next day. To his surprise, baby Paris was alive and well and being cared for by a family of bears. Agelaos believed that this was truly a sign from the gods, and he refused to kill the baby. In order to appease King Priam, he found a wild dog, killed it, and cut out its tongue to present to the king. Once the king was convinced that Paris was dead, Agelaos took Paris to secretly raise as his own son. He taught him to hunt and tend herds on the mountain slopes. Paris was strong and healthy and grew into a strikingly handsome, yet humble young man.

The *Iliad*—Section 2

The Wedding of King Pelias and Thetis the Sea Nymph

Back in Greece, King Pelias was taking Thetis the sea nymph as his bride. It was a magnificent wedding under the golden light of the full moon. Stars glimmered in the deep blue sky like sparkling confetti, and a ring of shining torches glowed where they hung among the olive branches.

Since Pelias and Thetis were prominent figures, both gods and mortals attended the grand wedding feast. The many guests strolled and mingled outdoors while nine muses serenaded the wedding party with their magical music. Handsome Ganymedes, cup-bearer to the gods, poured sweet nectar and ambrosia from his silver jugs. For the moment, peace reigned; Pelias and Thetis were in love.

However, not everyone was pleased. Eris, the goddess of strife and discord, was jealous and angry because she had not been invited to the wedding. She decided to go anyway. When she appeared, the music stopped and everyone turned to stare at the unwelcome guest. In her hand Eris held a beautiful golden apple. She lifted the apple aloft, then with a shrill and piercing laugh she tossed it onto the ground. It rolled around, winding its way through the crowd until it stopped at the feet of the three most powerful goddesses—Athena, the goddess of wisdom; Aphrodite, the goddess of love and beauty; and Hera, queen of the gods and wife to Zeus.

When the crowd looked back to Eris for an explanation, she was gone. King Pelias walked over and bent to pick up the apple. "Is it a present for us?" the goddesses asked (for they were quite vain).

King Pelias reached for the beautiful fruit, but as soon as he touched it, a cold chill ran down his spine. "How mysterious," said Athena. "What do you think it means?" King Pelias turned the apple over in his hands and discovered a small inscription that read "To the fairest." The goddesses began to question the king, "Well, to whom shall you give it? It was obviously intended for one of us." The crowd formed a large circle and chattered among themselves, speculating about what to do. King Pelias was now distraught on this most happy and cherished day. He grew silent and still, unable to act. Then Zeus, king of the gods, broke through the circle. "Tonight is not the time to decide who gets the apple. We are here to celebrate a wedding. Let us get on with the feast!"

The three goddesses began to bicker and argue amongst themselves about who was the fairest and who should get the apple. Finally Zeus could take it no longer. He interrupted them and proclaimed, "Paris, the true son of King Priam of Troy, will be the fair judge. It will be up to him to decide who gets the golden apple!" He then took the apple from Pelias and stepped back, but the happy atmosphere of the wedding had been lost. Clouds covered the moon and it grew cold.

The *Iliad*—Section 3

The Judgment of Paris

As dawn broke after the marriage of King Pelias, Zeus and the other gods returned to Mount Olympus. Zeus sent for his trusted messenger, Hermes, with the swift and winged feet. He instructed Hermes to accompany Athena (goddess of wisdom), Aphrodite (goddess of love and beauty), and Hera (Zeus's wife and queen of all the gods) to find Paris, so he could make the fateful decision about the golden apple.

Hermes flew along the Trojan coastline in search of Paris. He found the young man tending his flock. When Paris saw Hermes and the three goddesses, he began to run away. Hermes called out to him. "Do not fear what you see, herdsman Paris, for you have been chosen by Zeus, Lord of Olympus, to perform a great task. He has sent me here with these three goddesses for he knows of your courage and fairness of judgment." Paris was scared but also a bit intrigued.

Hermes and the goddesses approached Paris and presented him with the golden apple. They showed him the inscription and described the scene at the wedding. Hermes told him that it was Zeus's wish that he alone decide who should receive the coveted golden apple. Paris read the inscription aloud— "To the fairest"—and looked into the eager faces of the goddesses awaiting his decision. The magnitude of his task began to sink in.

Pulling Hermes aside, Paris confessed that he was frightened to make such a bold decision because one goddess was as fair as the other. After all, he was only a mortal. How could he escape the vengeance of the two goddesses who were not chosen? Hermes comforted Paris and promised that they would all abide by his decision because it was the will of Zeus. The three goddesses stepped forward and agreed with Hermes.

Hera was the first to speak on her behalf. "Choose me, gallant Paris, and you shall have powers far greater than that of any king. I will make you lord of all Asia and Greece." Paris thought about how his life would be different to be such a king. Perhaps his destiny was not that of a herdsman after all.

Athena broke the spell. "Power is good, fair Paris, yet what good is power without the wisdom to wield it properly? I will give you wisdom. You will be the wisest man on earth and everyone will seek you for your advice. It is with this knowledge that you will gain power, for you will be able to get anything your heart desires." Paris thought being the wisest man in the world seemed much better even than being a king.

Then beautiful Aphrodite looked deep into Paris's soul to find what he truly desired. She spoke with words like music, "Dear Paris, knowledge and power cannot give you what your lonely heart desires; they cannot give you love. If you choose me as the fairest, I will give you the most beautiful woman upon the earth to be your bride. Her name is Helen of Sparta." Paris's heart skipped a beat because this was the best offer of all. He immediately handed the golden apple to Aphrodite, who laughed triumphantly and promised to lead Paris to Helen in Greece.

Athena and Hera refused to accept this decision, believing that Paris had not judged fairly. They accused him of deciding on the basis of his own desires rather than who was truly the fairest. They stormed away angrily and vowed revenge.

The *Iliad*—Section 4

Paris Returns to Troy

Now that Aphrodite had promised Helen of Sparta would become Paris's wife, she told Paris that he would need to perform some deeds to prove that he was worthy. She also told him Helen was already married. She said, "Helen is the most beautiful and heavily guarded mortal in the world. King Menelaus, her husband, is very protective and jealous. Even if you do manage to steal her away, how do you expect to win her heart?" Paris understood his predicament.

It so happened that King Priam was sponsoring a competition inside the walls of Troy. A prize bull would be awarded to the man who could win the set of challenges. Paris begged his father, Agelaos, to let him enter the competition. Agelaos was torn. He knew that his son was really the son of the king and most able of all men in Troy. This meant that Paris would most likely win the competition, but it also meant that he might lose his adopted son forever.

Eventually, Agelaos agreed and escorted Paris into the walled city. Paris had never been inside Troy before. He was excited and awed as he joined the other men who were competing. Even Hector and Deiphobus, King Priam's other sons, had entered the competition, sure that they would be victorious.

Paris's strength and cunning overcame all obstacles, and he was declared the winner. King Priam's other sons refused to admit defeat, and at the end of the day when Paris was presented the prize bull, the two drew their swords and prepared to slay him. Quickly, Agelaos leapt in front of Paris and pleaded with the king. "Please, my lord, I beseech you. Do not let them kill this youth, for he is your true son, Paris!"

King Priam and Hecuba were overwhelmed. They welcomed Paris back into their family and proposed that he live with them in Troy as a prince. Eventually his brothers accepted him also. But their sister Cassandra did not welcome Paris at all. She was a prophetess and understood the disaster that was imminent now that Paris was back. She pleaded with her father to kill Paris, warning him that doom would surely befall Troy if Paris were allowed to live. King Priam only smiled and said, "It's better that Troy should fall than that I should lose this wonderful new son of mine!"

Paris and Helen

Paris, now a prince, was eager to claim Helen as his bride. With the help of Aphrodite he sailed across the Aegean Sea to Sparta. He came ashore with great tributes, tricking King Menelaus into believing that he was on a goodwill mission from his father. Helen and Paris spent much time together during his stay at the palace, and she fell in love with him. Aphrodite assured Paris that they would have a beautiful future together, free from revenge.

One night Paris stole Helen away and sailed back to Troy. During the voyage Hera created a great storm, determined to destroy them but they managed to sail through safely to Troy. The moment the Trojans laid eyes upon Helen they fell in love and worshipped her as their queen. Back in Greece, King Menelaus was filled with rage to find his wife gone. With the help of his brother Agamemnon, King of Mycenae, Menelaus raised an army larger than any before. Then they set out to conquer Troy and reclaim Helen.

The *Iliad*—Section 5

The Birth of Achilles

While Paris was in Sparta winning Helen, King Pelias and Thetis were having problems of their own. After the incident with the golden apple, the couple lived happily for a while with their family of daughters. But as the years passed, King Pelias grew more and more dejected, for although Thetis had given birth to six sons, each one had mysteriously died in infancy.

Thetis was despondent over the death of her baby sons. She secretly longed to return to the sea and the comfort of the waves. She no longer wanted to be queen; she wanted the simple life of a sea nymph once more. But as fate would have it, she had a seventh son, whom they named Achilles.

Determined not to lose this son, Thetis secretly vowed to make Achilles invulnerable. Without telling her husband, she took Achilles into the Underworld of the god Hades and dipped the baby in the River Styx. The river was swift and Thetis did not want to lose her baby, so she held him tightly by one heel. The magical protecting waters washed all over Achilles, except for the heel that his mother held.

Upon learning that Thetis had gone, King Pelias was distraught and suspicious. His wife had been acting strangely, and he was concerned for Achilles' safety. He was relieved when his wife and son returned unharmed, but he determined to keep a watchful eye on them. That night as Pelias pretended to be asleep, he saw Thetis remove Achilles from his cradle and place him in the fire that warmed their chambers. He quickly lunged out of bed and grabbed the baby out of the flames. "You fool!" cried Thetis. "Had you left Achilles in the flames he would have become immortal. He has been dipped in the River Styx and is invulnerable to the fire."

Achilles Grows Up

Thetis could take no more. Upset and cross, she left her husband and child and disappeared back into the sea, never to return. Pelias was distressed at the loss of his lovely wife. Because of his sorrow, he took Achilles up to Mount Pelion and turned him over to the care of a wise Centaur named Chiron. Chiron was entrusted by many fine families in Greece to raise their sons to become heroes. The Centaur loved Achilles and brought him up as if he were his own son. He fed him the flesh of mountain lions to give him courage and sweet honeycombs to make him run swiftly. Achilles was taught well in all areas, including music, healing, and athletics. He grew into a handsome youth with a mass of golden curls, and his skills were unsurpassed.

The *Iliad*—Section 6

The Trojan War Begins

As Achilles grew into a strong and vibrant youth atop Mount Pelion with Chiron the Centaur, the clouds of war were gathering throughout Greece. Warriors and princes assembled, preparing to sail in battle to Troy. Agamemnon organized the troops to defend his brother's honor and seek revenge. They met at the port of Aulis and over a thousand ships set sail.

Achilles had been isolated in the mountains and therefore had not been called upon to do battle. When he heard of the coming war, he immediately set out for Troy. Chiron presented the boy with a magic spear that would fight true for only him. He also gave him a mighty shield covered in ivory and jewels, and tunics and cloaks to protect him against the biting winds.

Achilles sought out his cousin Patroclus to join him on his journey. Patroclus was older but not nearly as skilled as the brave Achilles. Achilles loved his cousin more than anyone else in the world. While sailing across the Aegean, the two warriors encountered Thetis, the sea nymph and Achille's mother, who had left him as an infant. She warned them to let someone else land at Troy first because the first to set foot on Trojan soil would surely die.

As Achilles and Patroclus waited at the enemy coastline, the warning of Thetis came true. The first man to land was stabbed by Hector, the eldest prince of Troy. He was the main leader of the Trojan army throughout what was to become a long and bloody war. Agamemnon led the bravest of Greece's warriors into battle against Troy. But the Trojans were prepared. They held firm inside the walled city.

Achilles Meets Briseis and Withdraws from Battle

As the war continued, Achilles and his magic spear won battle after battle. His name became the most feared in the entire army. During a bold attack on the nearby city of Lyrnessus, Achilles met a beautiful princess named Briseis. He fell in love with this enchanting creature but could not make her his wife because she was Trojan. Instead, he took her back to his camp to be his serving maid.

Achilles did not get along particularly well with Agamemnon, the leader of the Greeks. Agamemnon was jealous of the notoriety Achilles was receiving, and soon they had an argument over Briseis. Agamemnon had found himself a beautiful captive, but he had been forced to send her back to Troy when it was discovered that she was a true priestess. Out of jealousy and spite, Agamemnon pulled rank on Achilles and took Briseis for himself. Achilles could not retaliate against his leader, so in anger and despair he stormed off to his tent and removed himself from the war. The future looked bleak for the Greek war effort.

At first the Greeks refused to believe that such a great warrior would sulk over a Trojan woman. But as the days passed, Achilles remained in his tent. Soon word traveled across Troy that the great Achilles had quit fighting. The Trojans returned to the battlefields with renewed hope. They knew they had a chance of defeating the enemy if they didn't have to face the invincible Achilles. Soon the Trojans gained the upper hand. In one fierce battle both Agamemnon and the King of Ithaca, Odysseus, were brutally wounded. Even with this news, Achilles would not leave his tent to help save the Greek army.

The *Iliad*—Section 7

Achilles Returns with a Vengeance

When Achilles lost his love, Briseis, to Agamemnon, he lost all will to fight, and the Greeks were devastated on the battlefields. It was Patroclus who finally saved the day. This brave cousin of Achilles was determined to turn away the Trojans. He ran forward dressed in Achilles' armor and hurled a spear into the Trojan masses. The deceit worked—the Trojans mistook Patroclus for Achilles and ran away in fear. Patroclus then led the Greek army and chased the Trojans all the way back to their walled city.

Word reached Achilles of his cousin's brave deed. He mustered his strength and gathered more forces to help his beloved Patroclus. It was too little, too late. Just as Achilles arrived on the battle scene, Patroclus took a blow between his shoulder blades that hurled him to the ground. Achilles ran over to help but was intercepted by Hector, who rode up and with one mighty blow killed Patroclus.

Achilles let loose with a chilling war cry. He reentered the battle full of grief and vengeance that knew no mercy. Eventually he was able to recover the body of Patroclus from the Trojans and give him a proper burial by the sea with full honors. Agamemnon brought Briseis to the funeral and made peace with Achilles. Standing beside his cousin's grave, Achilles vowed to avenge his cousin's death.

The Death of Hector

Up to this point Achilles and Hector had not faced each other on the battlefield. But now a deep hatred sweltered between them. Hector sent word to the Greek camp that he wished to challenge Achilles in single combat. Achilles willingly accepted.

It was a clear and sunny morning when the two soldiers faced each other amidst a crowd. Hector wore black and silver armor and carried a sword in one hand and a spear in another. Hearing of her son's challenge, Thetis visited Achilles in the night and presented him with a special suit of golden armor. As he stepped forward in it, the reflection of the sun almost blinded those standing nearby.

Achilles attacked, fiercely motivated by the memory of his dear cousin. Hector was the stronger of the two soldiers, but Achilles was far quicker and more agile. Suddenly a cry rang out amid the Trojans— Achilles had stabbed Hector through the heart.

As he crumpled to his knees Hector begged, "Please let my parents have my body to bury honorably." "Never!" cried Achilles as he viciously twisted his sword and watched the last glimmer of life leave Hector's eyes. Achilles then tied Hector's body to his chariot and dragged it in the dirt as he circled the walls of Troy. King Priam and the Trojans were horrified.

King Priam then went to Achilles and threw himself on the ground in front of the warrior. "You have proven to be a great warrior, now prove you are a great man. Return my son to Troy." Achilles, moved by this gesture, wept and gave orders to return the body to Troy. He then called for a truce to last twelve days so that Hector could have an honorable funeral.

The *Iliad*—Section 8

The Trojan Horse

For ten long years the bloody battle between Greece and Troy raged on. "The siege is not going well," thought Odysseus, hero and King of Ithaca. He wondered if the terrible death toll was too high for the rescue of one person. The person in question was Helen, the most beautiful woman in the world. It was for her and the honor of Greece that this war must end in victory. The Greeks thought long and hard about ways to end the war. Perhaps if they made special offerings to the gods, the gods might look favorably upon their gifts and reward them with the city of Troy.

Odysseus was struck by that idea—a gift! They would offer the Trojans a mysterious gift. They would build a huge and glorious wooden horse with a hollow belly. The horse would be left outside the gates of Troy as if it were a peace offering. Unknown to the Trojans, inside the horse's belly would be a Greek fighting force. When the magnificent beast was completed it was pulled into place outside the massive gates of Troy. That night, under the cover of darkness, a small band of chosen warriors hid inside. When dawn broke the next day, the rest of the Greeks made a big show of leaving sadly, as if in defeat. They boarded their ships and sailed away, leaving the horse behind as tribute to their victors.

The Trojans were overjoyed! With shouts of triumph they swarmed out of the city walls. For years they had been forced to stay inside, and now the land was theirs once more. But what was this horse? The Trojans were puzzled as to why the Greeks would build such a thing and then leave it behind. Was it a curse or a blessing? A Trojan priest approached the horse suspiciously. He walked around the giant steed admiring it, inspecting it, and finally rapping it with his staff. A hollow thud rang out. The sound sent chills through the priest. "I do not like this horse!" he cried to King Priam. "We must burn and destroy it, or else I fear it will destroy us!"

The people of Troy were frightened by the priest's words. They began to take measures to burn the wooden beast, and the soldiers inside feared for their lives. Then the gods interfered. Athena and Hera had vowed to punish Troy for the judgment of Paris. They could not let the Trojans win. They sent a huge serpent from the ocean onto the shore. The monstrous creature twined its poisonous coils around the sons of the priest. When he tried to save them, he too was killed. The people of Troy took this as a sign that the gods were not pleased with the priest's predictions, and they dragged the horse through the gates of their city as a symbol of their hard-won victory.

For hours the Trojans celebrated—drinking, feasting, and dancing. Later that night, when Troy was silent and still, the belly of the horse opened and the band of soldiers crept out. They quietly opened the gates to their army, which had sailed back during the night. The Greeks swept in and killed all who challenged them. King Priam was slain, and most of the women were taken as slaves. The Greeks had finally won the war! Helen was rescued and returned to Sparta and her husband, King Menelaus. Before sailing back to Greece, the Mycenaens made sure their victory was complete. They set fire to Troy. Hecuba's dream of giving birth to a flame that would destroy Troy had indeed come true. Because of Paris, her son, the city of Troy burned to the ground.

The Trojan Tabloid Times

After the class presentation of *The Iliad*, have the whole class or a small group of capable students put together a newspaper recounting the events of the tale. Below is a list of newspaper sections and suggested headlines. Assign an editor to organize the paper and arrange the articles into proper newspaper format. Then have some students illustrate some of the articles and write captions for them. Display the newspaper on a bulletin board or make copies to distribute. This is a fun way to check students' comprehension!

Main Stories/Current Events

- Queen Kidnapped from Home While Husband Sleeps
- UFO Spotted Over Trojan Mountains (Hermes and the Three Goddesses)
- Child Abuse Suspected by King Priam (or) Baby Raised by Bears
- I Married a Sea Nymph—Confessions of a Wedding Gone Wrong
- Baby Thrown Into Fire By Sea Nymph—"Unfit Mother" Claims King Pelias
- Giant Horse Presented to City
- Hecuba's Dream Comes True

Sports Section

- Mysterious Herdsman Battles the Princes of Troy in Series of Challenges
- Achilles vs. Hector—The Battle of Death
- The Contest of the Golden Apple—Athena vs. Hera vs. Aphrodite

Society Page

- Wedding of King Pelias and Thetis
- Welcome Home Celebration for Paris
- Victory Feast for Troy Gone Sour
- The Final Celebration in Greece—Send Our Troops Home!

The Classifieds

- Wanted: Greek Soldiers. Contact Agamemnon.
- Wanted: Achilles' magic spear. Contact Trojan Army.
- Wanted: Prophet to analyze Hecuba's dream. Contact King Priam.
- Wanted: Centaur to raise son. Contact King Pelias.
- Wanted: Trojan Serving Maid. Contact Achilles.
- For Sale: Golden Apple to highest bidder. Contact Paris.
- For Sale: Trojan Horse. Contact Odysseus.
- Classes offered in music and dancing. Contact Chiron the Centaur.

Birth Announcements

- Birth of Paris and Birth of Achilles

Obituaries

- Patroclus, Hector, Father of Briseis, and King Priam

Home Section

- Recipe for ambrosia and nectar by Ganymedes
- How to Build a Trojan Horse by Odysseus

44

Achilles Activities

Research Achilles' Death

Soon after the death of Hector, Achilles also met his demise. Have a group of students research how Achilles died. Have them present the information to the class in the form of a short drama.

What is Achillean?

The word "Achillean" is used in modern English and originates from the great Greek warrior Achilles. Have an individual or group of students use dictionaries to determine the meaning of "Achillean." Then have them present the meaning to the class by describing adjectives used in the definition and situations in which the word would be used properly.

Achilles' Tendon

What is the Achilles' tendon and why was it given this name? Have an individual or group of students look up the words in a dictionary. Then have them explain to the class what it is and how it refers to the story of Achilles.

Identify Your Achilles' Heel

One's Achilles' heel is that person's significant weakness—one that affects him or her adversely. Elicit from students how such a weakness got its name from Achilles (his mother's hand on his heel left it the only vulnerable spot on his body). Have students identify their personal weakness, or Achilles' heel. Perhaps they cannot refuse food (so they overeat). Perhaps they have to be the smartest (so they will even cheat). Maybe they have to be the most popular (so they are false friends). Have each write a brief and personal account of what he or she feels is his or her biggest weakness and how it affects choices and daily living. Allow volunteers to share their insights, but do not make sharing such private information mandatory.

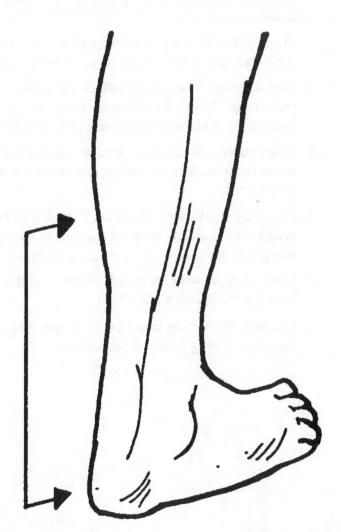

Write an Epic Story

Homer's tale of the Trojan War is filled with adventure, romance, and intrigue. Have your students create their own works of Greek literature, using the elements found in this traditional Greek story.

Preparing for the lesson:

1. Reproduce the Story Plot Outline (page 47) and the Editing Checklist (page 18) for each student.

2. Create an overhead transparency of the Story Plot Outline and The Writing Process (page 17).

3. Gather resource materials describing the different Greek gods and heroes for students to use as references.

Teaching the lesson:

1. Discuss the major elements found in Homer's *Iliad* that make it especially Greek. Elements might include the following: use of royalty—kings and queens; the common practice of having sons raised by someone else; mythical creatures such as the sea nymph, centaur, and serpent; use of magic; interference by the gods to cause obstacles in the plot; heroic qualities of main characters—beauty, strength, wisdom, cunning, humility, etc. Also note the references to ancient cities, landmarks, and geographical features of Greece, as well as food, clothing, and cultural clues.

2. Display The Writing Process transparency and review the steps. Tell students that they will create their own Greek Epic Story using elements found in the *Iliad*.

3. Distribute the Story Plot Outlines and explain to students that they will use this sheet for prewriting. Using the overhead transparency, review the sequence and sections of plot. Encourage students to keep their plots simple and focused on one main problem or conflict.

4. Brainstorm with the class possible conflicts, problems, and mythological creatures that might occur in a Greek story. Allow class time for students to complete their prewriting and write a rough draft.

5. Distribute the Editing Checklist to students and review how they should use it to improve their rough drafts. Allow time for students to work with peer editors to edit and revise their compositions.

6. Have students write their final drafts. Display the stories, make them into picture books, or combine them into a class book.

7. Evaluate the writing based on the proper sequence of story plot and the use of elements in Greek literature, giving feedback to students.

Story Plot Outline

I. Introduction

   A. Character descriptions _____

        _____

   B. Setting descriptions _____

        _____

   C. Problems or conflicts to be resolved by the end _____

        _____

II. Plot—Sequence of Events

   A. Obstacles/scenes leading to the climax

      1. _____

         _____

      2. _____

         _____

      3. _____

         _____

   B. Climax—the scene where the problem is solved—peak of excitement _____

        _____

        _____

III. Conclusion/Resolution

_____

_____

_____

_____

Acremedes the Assemblyman

Narrators 1—10	Xenos, Plutarch,
Acremedes	and Damian, his sons
Diedre, his wife	Sophles, Chintron,
Daldes, his father	and Hector, his friends

Narrator 1: The Dark Age came to an end around 750 B.C. Cities began to grow and trade increased. Leaders stepped forward in each region to organize and govern. Over the years many changes took place before democracy reigned in Greece. Let's listen as Acremedes and his family and friends tell us how the government of Greece evolved.

Acremedes: Welcome to my humble home. My father was just telling our three sons about life in Athens, our **city-state**, long ago. Once the Dark Age ended and trade increased once again, over 100 self-governing regions, or city-states, were established throughout Greece. Each had its own specific characteristics. A region was called a *polis*. Each polis consisted of the city and its surrounding rural area. For example, the polis of Athens included the walled city plus the surrounding area in Attica.

Narrator 2: We use the word "polis" today in many forms. For example, a metropolis is a large city or center of population and culture. The word "politics" means the art of governing a state. And when someone is considered "cosmopolitan" it means that they are very worldly, or at home in any country or culture.

Diedre: Of course, not every polis was equal in terms of natural resources. The lack of farmland caused many people to move into regions away from the mainland and begin other Greek colonies. Some city-states battled each other for land control then—and still do today. Grandfather Daldes was just telling the boys how government began with the kings and queens of Greece.

Daldes: Before the Dark Age, each area was ruled by powerful kings each of whom was usually the head of the area's richest family. Tales of these kings and their families abound in our Greek literature.

Narrator 3: This system of government was known as a monarchy, or "rule by one." In a monarchy, the king has ultimate power and control over the people in his area. He alone controls all of the land and natural resources of the region, and he is responsible for all decisions pertaining to his people. Another feature of a monarchy was that when the king died, the power would be handed down to his eldest son, thereby keeping the power in the family.

Damian: But how could one king defend an entire area? What if the people did not like the decisions he was making?

Acremedes the Assemblyman *(cont.)*

Daldes: The kings would rely on other wealthy families and nobles to help, in return for favors. Naturally, these families soon wanted a share of the power as well. By the end of the Dark Age, many city-states were governed by small groups of nobles who shared equal power. This was better than giving ultimate power to one man alone but still not satisfactory for the majority of the population.

Narrator 4: When a few people govern or hold power over a larger group of people it is known as an **oligarchy,** or "rule by a few." Many city-states, such as Sparta, continued to use this system, never fully evolving into a democracy. In an oligarchy there was a council made up of aristocrats, or those who were considered the "best people." Policies were then carried out by a higher lever of magistrates within the council.

Xenos: The leaders of the oligarchies must have improved conditions in their areas. Why didn't the oligarchies prevail?

Daldes: Different problems arose in the various city-states. Some regions grew too big and couldn't provide food for the population. People grew unhappy and decided to overthrow the leaders. New leaders emerged who promised to make things better. They convinced others to join in their fight and seized power by force. Once they had reformed the government, they ruled single-handedly.

Narrator 5: One who assumes ultimate power by force is known as a **tyran**t, or "ruler who governs in a harsh way"; a dictator. Their government was known as a tyranny. Many tyrants were liked because they let the people have a say in how the government would be changed and made more fair for all of the people, not just the aristocrats. Other tyrants were harsh and greedy, however, imposing severe laws and punishments. Many times the people of a polis would throw out one tyrant and replace him with another.

Plutarch: If one man had ultimate control again, how was this any different from the monarchies?

Daldes: The monarchy was run by a family. This family was not chosen by the people. A tyrant was supported or thrown out by the will of the population. This was a great step towards **democracy** because it taught the people of Greece that they could make changes in the government by uniting behind a chosen leader. In fact, when the last tyrant was thrown out of Athens, the people got together and decided to share the decision-making power among themselves. Thus the first democracy was born.

Narrator 6: "Democracy" comes from two Greek words: *demos*, meaning "people," and *kratos*, meaning "rule." Democracy meant "rule by the people." From about 500 B.C. and forward, Athens has been a democracy. Pericles, a famous Greek statesman, led Athens to the pinnacle of democratic government during the Golden Age of Athens.

Plutarch: I guess we always take our government for granted here in Athens, yet we must thank all of the people who came before us who made our good fortune possible. Father, can we head over to the Agora now? I believe there is to be a big trial today, and I was hoping we could go watch the debates.

Diedre: Yes, dear. Take the boys for a firsthand lesson in government. I will prepare the evening meal for your return. I will want to hear all about the happenings in the Agora today when you come home!

Acremedes the Assemblyman *(cont.)*

Narrator 7: Although Athens claimed to be a democracy, the citizens making the decisions comprised only about 15% of the total population. This included all adult males over 18 years of age born in the area. Only men could take part in public life. Women and girls stayed at home, going out only to enjoy the arts, such as the theater. They gained their social status from their husbands and male relatives. Even though women and children comprised 48% of the population, they had no political rights and could not own land. But they were protected under the law. Women saw their role in the home as an important one, and they were respected and honored by their husbands and families. Women were encouraged to be intelligent, strong-willed, and courageous, as well as gentle, loving, and talented in the arts.

Acremedes: Come, boys, we're off to the Agora. Who can tell me about the citizens of Athens?

Xenos: The citizens of Athens make the laws, hold trials at the assembly, and make all decisions regarding the workings of Athens. But not all men are considered citizens. Some are foreigners, or **metics**. Metics live and work in Athens but were born outside the city. Metics are protected by the law, but, like women, they cannot participate in government or own land.

Narrator 8: Metics paid taxes and served in the army. Life was not bad for these foreigners who comprised 12% of the population. Many of them had left their own polis in search of work and a better life. They were shopkeepers, craftsmen, and moneylenders. Most metics were highly respected within the community.

Damian: And don't forget the **slaves**—25% of the people who live in Athens. Some slaves are purchased from slave traders and some are prisoners of war. They are not considered citizens, but like Athenians, they are protected by laws. Still, they cannot vote, choose their own jobs, or even have families without the permission of their owners.

Plutarch: This is true, but most slaves are treated well. Many have been set up in business by their masters, who claim a share of their profits. Some work on the farms and some in households. Some slaves earn wages and can save money to buy their freedom.

Acremedes: Very good, boys! I can tell you have been taking our government lessons seriously. Ah, I see my three friends on the far side as we enter the **Agora** now. I think they have just come from the assembly and can tell you what a trial is like.

50

Acremedes the Assemblyman *(cont.)*

Narrator 9: The **Agora** was a large public meeting place in the center of the town. Here all of the citizens of Athens would gather to listen to the happenings of their polis. Men would discuss politics, philosophy, and business. Groups would gather around speakers attempting to persuade voters before entering the assembly. The Agora was usually a bustle of activity.

Sophles: Greetings! I see you have brought the boys along to experience today's follies in the Agora. I'm sure you have many questions about the workings of our politics, since one day you will each be a citizen entrusted with many duties.

Xenos: There are many people from all over Attica. The assembly of jurors and council members must consist of at least 6,000 citizens. But how does the assembly decide who will be a council member and who will be a juror for the trials?

Chintron: The region of Attica is divided into ten tribes. Each tribe sends 50 citizens to make up the council of 500. Then, each tribe takes turns running the assembly.

Hector: Thousands of jurors are summoned from all over Attica. They are paid by the government so that they can afford to take off from work. This way, rich or poor, every male citizen can take part in the government. It is very interesting to get all of these men together, for we can see that there are vast differences between those who live in the city and those who live in the country.

Plutarch: Yes, but isn't that the point of our government? To let all points of view be heard and allow all of the people a fair say in the decisions of the polis? I think it is a marvelous system!

Damian: I agree and would like to know more details. Exactly what happens inside the assembly at a trial?

Sophles: Every trial has hundreds of jurors. Each juror is given two disks—one to show for a vote of guilty and the other for vote of innocence. People on trial speak in their own defense in front of the assembly. They may also ask other citizens to speak on their behalf to help persuade the jurors. They are timed using a water clock so that each speaker gets an equal time to present their case. Once all speakers have been heard, which often can take several days, the jurors place one vote disk into a jar. The votes are counted and revealed. Punishments are then imposed.

Narrator 10: In Athens there were no judges or lawyers. Citizens had to plead their own case in front of hundreds of onlookers. If the case involved a woman, metic, or slave, a citizen was required to speak on his or her behalf, since these groups were not allowed to directly take part in the process. The ability of a speaker to be persuasive often accounted for a vote of innocence. A good speaker could sway the juror to his side regardless of the facts. Sometimes an assembly would change a verdict after realizing that they had been persuaded to make a rash decision.

Xenos: Father, what are those slaves doing over there?

Acremedes: They carry the rope and red paint to mark anyone who seems to be trying to avoid their assembly duties. A democracy can only work if everyone does his part. It is important that you understand and accept this great responsibility, because soon you will be a vital part of it. Never forget that participating in government is also a privilege that many people do not enjoy.

Plutarch: Thank you for this valuable lesson. I can't wait to grow up and become an assemblyman myself.

Acremedes the Assemblyman—
Vocabulary and Comprehension

The following words from the story can be used by students in their Vocabulary Journals (page 5). Remind students to write a complete definition of each word and illustrate them if they wish.

city-state	oligarchy	metic
polis	tyrant	slave
monarchy	democracy	Agora

All or some of the following questions can be used for whole class discussion, small group work, or individual assessment. Allow students to refer back to the passage while working.

1. Why did people move throughout Greece and away from the mainland after the Dark Age? *(There was competition for farmland and other natural resources.)*

2. Why didn't the original monarchies survive? *(The kings needed to rely on other wealthy families to help protect the region. Eventually these families also wanted part of the decision-making power.)*

3. Why did some Greeks prefer being ruled by a tyrant? *(Some tyrants promised to make life better for the poor and allowed the people a say in the decisions being made.)*

4. Who was considered a citizen in Athens, having the privilege to participate in government? *(Only males over 18 years of age who were born in the Athens region were citizens.)*

5. Was this an example of true majority rule? Why or why not? *(No, because the males over 18 and born in Athens were a minority of the population—about 15%.)*

6. How was a trial in Ancient Athens different from one today? *(There were no lawyers or judges. A citizen spoke on his own behalf or on the behalf of a woman, metic, or slave. The jury consisted of hundreds of people rather than just 12, and only men could serve on the jury.)*

The Evolution of Democracy in Athens

Use the chart below to describe the changes in government in Athens. In the boxes, write a description of the system named and tell why it didn't last.

monarchy	**Description:**
Monarchies didn't last because	

↓

oligarchy	**Description:**
Oligarchies didn't last because	

↓

tyranny	**Description:**
Tyrannies didn't last because	

↓

democracy	**Description:**

Comparing the Population

As a class, discuss the different rights and privileges of the Athenian population. Fill in the following chart based on your findings, then make a circle graph using a calculator and protractor to show the different proportions of the population out of the whole.

	Are protected by law	Can vote	Can own land	Can choose occupation	Can earn wages	% of population	% of 360° (% X 360°)
male citizens							
women and children							
metics							
slaves							
					Totals	<u>100%</u>	<u>360</u> °

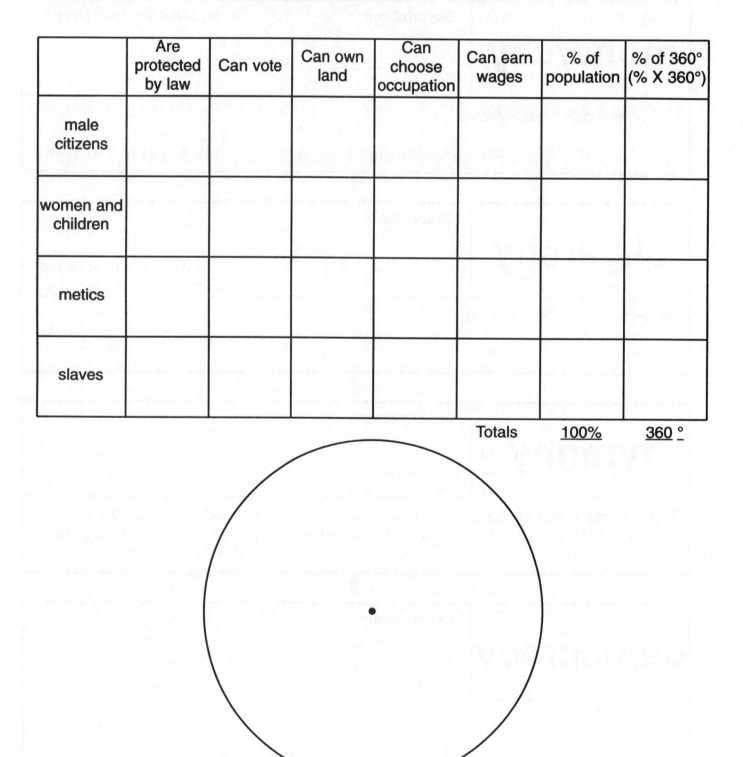

54

Form a City-State

To reinforce the workings of Athenian democracy, have students simulate Athenian society for a week.

Preparing for the lesson:

1. Divide the class into cooperative groups of about six to eight students. Make sure each group has boys and girls with a variety of learning abilities.

2. Move the groups of students' desks together to make tables for the groups to "live" for the week. This will represent their city-state, or polis.

3. Prepare a poster-board chart of the Rules of Athenian Democracy (page 56) to display throughout the week.

4. Gather materials for students to create a sign for their polis, and a chart showing their ten laws.

5. Make a chart on the chalkboard or poster board to show the name of each polis and to record the groups' points for each day.

Teaching the lesson:

1. As students enter the classroom, direct them to their desks, which are in a different location and configuration. Tell them that they will live in their "polis" for one week. Class will proceed as usual, with a few changes in duties and rules.

2. Explain that each day their group's polis will be awarded 15 points—10 points for "work" tasks and 5 points for "home" tasks. Display the point chart and tell students that each polis can earn up to 60 points (15 for each of four days). The polis's with the most points at the end of the week get to choose a special activity (watch a video about Greece, participate in an art activity or sporting event, longer recess, etc.) for the class.

3. Elicit from the class their agreement to follow the rules of Athenian democracy for a week. THEN tell them that this means that girls are responsible for the home tasks and boys are responsible for the work tasks and decision making. Reassure them that this will be fun and interesting, even though it may seem unfair at times.

4. Tell students that each day they will be assigned a polis work task and a home task that must be completed by the end of the day to keep their 15 points. Explain that they will NOT be given class time to work on these tasks. If the home task is not completed the whole 5 points will be lost and may not be made up. If the daily work task is not completed, the points for the day will be eliminated. If a work task is finished late, points may be made up, but the polis will lose 2 points for each day it is late. For example, if Day 1 work task is completed on Day 2, then only 8 points are scored for Day 1.

Form a City-State *(cont.)*

5. Display and discuss the following Rules of Athenian Democracy.

   • Men are responsible for all decision-making and all work. (Boys only participate in discussions or complete the daily work tasks assigned. Boys turn in papers for the group, get supplies, sharpen pencils, escort girls, etc. 10 points; deduct 2 points each time not followed.)

   • Women must always be accompanied by a man when entering and leaving their polis and the building. (All girls must be escorted to and from recess, bathroom, drinking fountain, office, etc. Deduct 2 points each time not followed.)

   • Women are responsible for the care of the home. (Girls are responsible for making sure that the polis is kept clean and tidy. They are to check and make sure each desk is neat on the inside as well as the outside. Deduct full 5 points if not followed.)

6. Each day assign one of the following tasks:

   Day 1: Work: Decide on a name for your polis and write it on the point chart.
   Home: Keep polis clean. (Do not deduct points on Day 1.)

   Day 2: Work: Make and hang a colorful sign on your table showing the name of your polis.
   Home: Keep polis clean.

   Day 3: Work: Make and display a chart listing 10 laws of your polis.
   Home: Keep polis clean.

   Day 4: Work: Tell one of the boys in the group that he has broken his polis's law, and choose the law from his chart. Tell the others that they must serve as jury for the trial of this person and come up with a verdict and punishment.
   Home: Keep polis clean.

   Day 5: Tally up points, declare a winner or winners, and allow them to choose an activity. Then lead a class discussion about what they learned and how they felt living a week in Ancient Athens.

   • Even though the girls may not have the freedom boys did, they also did not have the extra responsibilities of making decisions and laws.

   • How did the actions of just the boys affect the whole group?

   • How did the actions of just the girls affect the whole group?

   • How do they feel about the division of labor and decision making based on gender?

   • Do the girls feel that the laws written by the boys were fair?

   • How did the law-breaker feel that the jury treated him? Were they fair? Why or why not?

   • What ways would they change things to create a more true democracy?

Athenian Courtroom Drama: Arcades and Erin

Simulate a trial during an assembly in Ancient Athens.

Preparing for the lesson:

1. Choose four persuasive students to play the parts of the speakers during the trial: Arcades and Davian for one side, Zephre and Parthon for the other.

2. Make four copies of The Story of Arcades and Erin (pages 58 and 59) and two copies of Points to Make During the Trial (pages 60 and 61).

3. Gather voting tokens (colored cubes, checkers, beans, etc.) for the rest of the class, who will act as jurors. Each student will need one token that represents a guilty verdict and one that represents an innocent verdict.

4. Gather a box or containers for casting the votes. Make sure you cannot see the inside of the containers. Label one container "Guilty" and the other "Innocent."

Teaching the lesson:

1. Tell the class they will he holding a mock trial in the manner of the Ancient Greeks. Explain that you have chosen the four speakers and that the rest of them will be the all-important jury.

2. Tell the four speakers that they will present their cases in front of the class. Distribute and read The Story of Arcades and Erin with them. Tell them that the rest of the class will NOT hear this version of the story and that they are not to tell anyone before the trial. The only information the class will get regarding the situation is the charge brought by Zephyr, Erin's father, and the information the speakers present.

3. Meet with each side of the case and discuss their strategy for persuading the jurors by reviewing the appropriate Points to Make During the Trial. Tell them that they each will have three minutes ONLY to present their speeches, so it is important that they work together to cover their points adequately and persuasively to the jury. Tell them they will be cut off at three minutes regardless of whether or not they have finished their speeches.

4. Allow the speakers a few days to write and practice their presentations. You may want to review them to ensure the information is accurate.

5. On the day of the "trial," select one student to act as the timer and two students to act as the vote counters. Distribute the voting tokens to students and tell them which one represents a vote of guilty and which one represents a vote of innocence. Review the trial procedure (page 62).

6. Before beginning, remind students that they are to pretend that they are all male citizens of Athens. They are to listen to the facts presented during the speeches and analyze them from a Greek perspective. Remind them of the Ancient Greek custom allowing only male children to work and earn wages for the family. Therefore, it was important for a family to have boys to help with the business and support the family. Girls stayed at home and helped with the chores. However, it was customary that when a girl married, her family paid the husband a dowry, or sum of money. So not only does a girl cost her family money because she cannot work, she also costs her family money when she marries. This is why it was within the law and a typical practice to leave a baby girl or an unhealthy baby outside the city walls in hopes that someone wanting a child would adopt it. It was also legal and a typical practice for a man to divorce a wife who does not bear a son, in hopes of finding another wife who will.

7. Use Erin's Family vs. Arcades (page 62) to introduce and direct the action of the trial.

Athenian Courtroom Drama *(cont.)*

The Story of Arcades and Erin

Arcades was 33 years old when he finally took a wife. The marriage was arranged with a family that he had known for many years. Zephre, the head of the girl's family, approached him and proposed that his youngest daughter, Erin, would make a good and capable wife for Arcades. Arcades had known Erin since she was a small child, but it had been many years since their paths had crossed. His sisters told him that Erin had grown into a beautiful woman of fifteen and that her family had become wealthy.

The wedding arrangements were made without Arcades and Erin seeing each other or speaking. The ceremony took place, and as was customary, a dowry was paid. The amount was considerable since her family had recently prospered. Arcades was extremely pleased at his good fortune. He now had a beautiful and pleasant wife, as well as some money to expand his business.

Some time later, Erin became a pregnant and gave birth to a beautiful baby girl. Arcades was disappointed at not having a son to help with the family business, but the baby was beautiful and brought much joy to him and Erin. Besides, there was still plenty of time for Erin to have a boy, and soon his disappointment was forgotten. Erin proved to be a good mother and an excellent wife. She managed the home well, was assertive yet courteous with the slaves, and was always good company to come home to after a hard day's work.

Erin again became pregnant. Arcades looked forward to the birth of a son, but once again the baby was a girl. This time Arcades could not hide his disappointment. He worried about the future and the cost of providing dowries for his daughters to marry. How could he manage this without a son to help with the work? He knew that it was common practice to abandon an unwanted child outside the city gates. People unable to have children of their own might adopt the child and raise her as their own. Arcades gave serious consideration to this plan.

The day after the birth, he visited Erin and the new baby. As soon as Erin saw her husband she knew what he intended to do. Arcades took one look at his wife and thought of how loyal and devoted she had been these past years. He saw the despair in her eyes at the thought of losing her baby, and he could not bring himself to abandon the child. He felt that he was being foolish for making this decision, since most Athenians would not have considered keeping a second girl unless they were very wealthy. Erin was delighted to keep the baby. On the fifth day religious rites were performed, and on the tenth day the baby was named. Erin could rest at ease, for now the baby was an official part of the family and could not be rejected.

Three years later Erin became pregnant again. This was a time for great concern. Arcades' business had not been going well. If Erin did not have a boy this time, there was little doubt as to what would happen. Throughout the pregnancy the marriage began to change. Arcades became more obsessed with the business and worried about the family's future. He came home less frequently, and Erin became worried and unhappy.

When the third girl was born, Arcades did not even visit his wife. Instead he sent a message to her demanding that the baby be packed up and left outside the city gates. Erin had no choice but to obey her husband. She prayed and made offerings in hopes that the gods would find suitable parents for her baby and let her live. Erin knew she would never learn the fate of her child, and alone in her bedroom chambers she wept.

Athenian Courtroom Drama (cont.)

The Story of Arcades and Erin

From that time on the marriage was never the same. Erin and Arcades lost the close relationship they once had. Now they rarely had contact with one another, and Erin feared what would happen. Arcades soon decided to divorce her. He felt that she had been cursed by the gods and would only bring him more misfortune. Why else would his business be failing and his wife only bear girls? He felt that he must find himself another wife who could change his fate and bear him sons, or his family would perish.

Divorces happened quickly in Athens, so soon the arrangements were made. Erin's older brother, Parthon, was asked to come to the house and witness the divorce. Arcades also asked his good friend Davian to be a witness. When everyone was assembled, Arcades explained his predicament and read a statement of formal divorce. Erin was then asked to leave the house with her brother and rejoin her birth family. As was customary, their two daughters remained with Arcades. Arcades then took steps to find a new wife to help raise his daughters and, with luck, give birth to a son.

All of this was carried out in a correct way according to the law. But Arcades did not return the dowry to Erin's family after the divorce. He told himself that he didn't have the money because his business wasn't doing well, and taking out such a large sum would surely ruin him. If his business failed, how could he eventually pay the dowries for his and Erin's daughters? Arcades loved his daughters and felt that since it was Erin who was cursed to bear girls, it was her family's obligation to let him keep the money and provide for their futures. Therefore, instead of visiting Erin's family to negotiate some type of repayment, he ignored them, hoping that with his new wife all would come right in the end.

Erin's family felt hurt and wronged. They did not realize that Arcades had been having such difficulty with his business. Erin was distraught at losing her family and blamed herself. Zephre and Parthon talked the matter over and decided to bring Arcades to trial. They knew that there was nothing that they could do about the divorce, since it was legal. They also knew that they could not get Erin's children back unless Arcades allowed it. But they could force him to return the dowry, because Athenian law required the dowry to be returned along with the wife. And so it was that Arcades was brought to trial by Erin's family, accused of illegally keeping Erin's dowry and asking the jury to demand its repayment.

Tips for Writing the Speeches

Arcades: You are the accused husband. You will defend your position and justify your actions for keeping the dowry.

Davian: You are a good friend of Arcades. You will speak on his behalf. You should describe the good character of Arcades, his integrity, and his need to do the best for his children and their future.

Zephre: You are Erin's father. Concentrate on your legal right to have the full amount of the dowry returned. You can also solicit the sympathy of the jury for your daughter, who has lost her family, home, and husband.

Parthon: You are Erin's brother. Erin cannot speak for herself since she is a woman. You should describe the good character of your sister as a worthy wife and devoted mother. You can also explain your family needs the dowry to now support your sister, who has come home.

Athenian Courtroom Drama *(cont.)*

Points to Make for Arcades to Keep the Dowry

Arcades and Davian, you should retell the entire story from YOUR perspective and emphasize these points to the jury:

1. You were happy about the arranged marriage and assumed you had made a good choice. However, you soon learned that the family had tricked you into taking Erin, for they surely knew that she was cursed. That was why they paid you such a large dowry in the first place.

2. Your wife proved to be a bad omen—three daughters and no sons to help with the business. You were foolish but kind-hearted to keep the second child and had no other choice but to abandon the third. Any intelligent Athenian would have to agree.

3. With no sons to help with the business, you were soon having difficulty supporting the family and saving for two dowries. If the dowries could not be large, there would be no hope of finding good families for your daughters to marry into. Your wife was certainly cursed for bringing such misfortune, and her family knew of this and tried to deceive you.

4. You love your daughters more than anything and are only thinking of their futures. Erin changed after the birth of the third child, and it was obvious that she was no longer a fit wife or good mother. She also knew by now that she was cursed and was hurting her own family. Therefore, you had no choice but to ask for a divorce, remarry, and hope that a new wife could wipe away the curse and bring prosperity back into your home by bearing you a son. This was the only possible course of action given the circumstances of the marriage.

5. Therefore the dowry not only CANNOT but SHOULD NOT be repaid.

   • Your business cannot afford the loss of such a large sum of money. The business will fail and your daughters will suffer. Even giving back the daughters to Erin is no guarantee that they will prosper, because Erin is cursed and will not be easy to marry off again.

   • The dowry money was given to provide for his wife and offspring. His wife did not hold up her end of the bargain and have sons, so now the money has been all used up on her daughters. Raising a family of only girls is very costly. The money was not wasted but used to provide for the family and run the business with no other help.

   • If sons had been born they could have helped in the business and could have married and received their own dowry. Daughters are only a burden. They cannot help with the work and they need money for future dowries. If the money is forced to be paid back, you will ruin Arcades and put his—and Erin's—daughters at risk of living in poverty and never marrying at all.

Athenian Courtroom Drama *(cont.)*

Points to Make for Arcades to Return the Dowry

Zephre and Parthon, you retell the entire story from YOUR perspective and emphasize these points to the jury.

1. You were happy about the marriage and thought Arcades would be a good provider. You gave a large dowry in good faith that it would be used wisely and provide a nice nest egg to increase his family's business and make the family prosperous. The money must have been squandered to have disappeared so quickly.

2. Erin was a good wife and mother. She was not cursed. The fact that she had only daughters was not her fault. In fact, Arcades was doing so poorly in business that it must be he who was cursed and destined to failure.

3. By the third pregnancy the marriage changed. Erin tried her best but Arcades was no longer a fit husband. He came home less and ignored the needs of his family. It is obvious that he doesn't really care for his daughters and wants to keep them only as a reason to not repay the dowry. Is this a good father?

4. Imagine Erin's sorrow after trying her hardest to please her family and then having a third daughter. She was and still is distraught over placing the baby outside the gates hoping that some kind family would adopt it. She knew that she was actually abandoning the child to die. What a wicked and shameful father and husband to order such an action!

5. This is a man only concerned with money and not the future of his family. We cannot dispute the divorce. But a man of good character would have made some effort to negotiate payment instead of refusing to speak to the family. Erin needs another chance to find a suitable husband who is a fit provider and good businessman, one who is not surrounded by such bad omens from the gods. She has proven to be a devoted mother and dutiful wife who would be an asset for any husband.

6. Erin wants her daughters. We know that this is not the decision of the court and we can only plead our case to Arcades. But for Erin to find a suitable new husband to provide for her and her daughters, it is imperative that the full amount of the dowry be returned.

   - Only then can Erin remarry and get her daughters back because certainly selfish Arcades will not want the girls without the money.

   - We were once open to the idea of negotiating a payment over time. However, Arcades refused any contact with our family. Now it is too late. Full payment is required when returning a wife to the family after the divorce. We are only asking for the law to be upheld.

   - If Arcades' business fails, it is only his own doing for being such a poor businessman. We entrusted him to use the money wisely to provide for Erin and their children, but he failed at that, too.

Athenian Courtroom Drama *(cont.)*

Erin's Family vs. Arcades

Teacher/Council Member: Jurors, you have been selected to serve in today's trial, and I ask that you listen carefully to the proceedings. Each of you as a citizen of Athens must perform your duty to uphold the law and promote a better future for our polis. You have each been given two tokens with which to vote. Two jurors have been selected to count the votes. Will you please stand? (The two students comply.) Thank you. This is a container for your vote. You may cast only one vote—either guilty or innocent. (Point out the container.)

Will the timekeeper please stand. (The student assigned as the timer complies.) I request that you attend to the clock at this time. Before we begin today's proceedings, I must warn you that I will have silence during this trial. Any offender will be harshly removed.

The case before you today has been brought by Zephre, the father of Erin, divorced wife of Arcades. Zephre claims that Arcades has broken the law by returning Erin to her family without also returning the substantial dowry paid at the wedding. He asks the court to find Arcades guilty and to force the return of said money in full payment. I call on Zephre to present his case. Timekeeper, please start the clock.

Zephre speaks. Regardless of whether he finishes or not, time is called at three minutes.

Teacher/Council Member: Thank you, Zephre. You may be seated. I now call on Arcades to speak on his own behalf.

Arcades speaks. Regardless of whether he finishes or not, time is called at three minutes.

Teacher/Council Member: Thank you. Please step down, Arcades. I now call on Parthon, son of Zephre and brother of Erin, who wishes to speak on behalf of his sister and father.

Parthon speaks. Regardless of whether he finishes or not, time is called at three minutes.

Teacher/Council Member: Thank you. I now call on our final speaker, Davian, who wishes to speak on behalf of his friend Arcades.

Davian speaks. Regardless of whether he finishes or not, time is called at three minutes.

Teacher/Council Member: Thank you, Davian. Members of the jury, you have heard the evidence given by both sides in this case. Think carefully about this evidence and the consequences of your vote. Remember, we are ONLY deliberating whether or not Arcades should return the dowry. No other actions should be considered. If you vote guilty (hold up a "guilty" token), you are stating that Arcades should return the money. If you vote innocent (hold up the "innocent" token), you are stating that Arcades does not have to return the money. Please cast your votes. (Have students take turns walking to the container and placing one of their tokens inside.)

Thank you, jurors. I will now ask that the votes be counted and the verdict delivered. (Have the two students count the tokens in the containers and deliver the verdict.) While votes are being counted read aloud The Story of Arcades and Erin (pages 58 and 59) to the whole class.

Lead a discussion about the verdict, the strengths and weaknesses of the Ancient Athenian system of law, Erin's feelings at not being able to speak on her own behalf, and having an all-male jury. Discuss the feelings of the students taking part in the case. What issues did it raise for them? Talk about why students voted as they did and who was the most persuasive speaker.

Comparing Democracy

Use the Venn diagram to show similarities and differences between Ancient Athens and the United States today. Write the letter of each phrase in the appropriate place on the diagram.

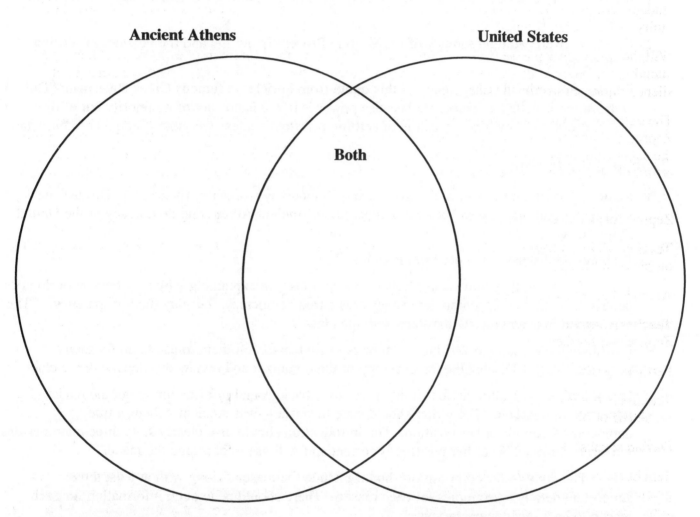

Ancient Athens   **United States**

Both

A. women can work and own property

B. women are politically active

C. over 100 jurors per trial

D. everyone is protected by the law

E. both sides in a trial are allowed to speak

F. women cannot vote

G. foreigners cannot vote

H. women not politically active

I. foreigners can become citizens and vote

J. an accused person represents himself at trial

K. women can vote

L. citizens can speak out freely

M. women cannot work or own property

N. judge and lawyers at trial

O. citizens must be born in the area

P. any citizen can hold a government position

Q. opportunity to better your position in life

R. jury of 12 people

Persuasive Writing

Have students demonstrate their understanding of Athenian government by writing a persuasive composition and following up with persuasive speeches or a class debate.

Preparing for the lesson:

1. Reproduce a Persuasive Writing Organizer (page 65) and Editing Checklist (page 18) for each student.

2. Create an overhead transparency of the Writing Process (page 17) and the Persuasive Writing Organizer.

3. Prepare an overhead transparency of this quote from Pericles, a famous Greek statesman: "Our constitution is called a democracy because power is in the hands not of a minority but of the whole people. When it is a question of settling private disputes, everyone is equal before the law."

Teaching the lesson:

1. Review student's responses to the Comparing Democracy worksheet (page 63). Discuss the similarities and differences between democracy in Ancient Athens and democracy of the United States today.

2. Display and discuss the quote from Pericles.

3. Tell students that they will write a persuasive composition explaining why they believe or do not believe that Ancient Athenian democracy was a true democracy. Display the transparency of The Writing Process and review the steps with the class.

4. Distribute the Persuasive Writing Organizers to students. Tell them to use them for their prewriting stage. Display the transparency of the organizer and review the steps with the class.

   Introduction: The introduction should give some background information to get the reader interested in the topic. The writer should state the issue—was Ancient Athens a true democracy—and his or her position. The introduction should also clearly state three main reasons the writer believes his or her position is correct and will use to persuade the reader.

   Body: The body of the composition should include the reasons along with at least three supporting details or examples for each reason. There should be enough information for each reason to be a separate paragraph.

   Conclusion: The conclusion should briefly restate or summarize the reasons for the writer's position. It also needs to include a convincing and persuasive closing statement.

5. Allow time for students to complete their rough drafts. Then distribute an Editing Checklist to each student and review how to use the checklist to improve their compositions.

6. Once students have completed their final drafts, share compositions and note which position is the most popular.

7. As an extension to the writing activity, have students pick a current issue for a persuasive speech. Have students give their speeches to the class as if they were at the Agora. Or choose a controversial topic and lead a class debate.

Persuasive Writing Organizer

Introduction (Tell background information, the issue, your position on the issue, and three main reasons for your position) _____

_____

_____

_____

Reason #1	Supporting Details
Reason #2	
Reason #3	

Conclusion (Summarize your reasons and give a convincing closing statement.)

_____

_____

_____

_____

Triton the Trader

The mountainous terrain in Greece made travel by land very difficult. Therefore, the sea become Greece's main highway for travel, trade, and conquest. Join Triton, a typical Athenian tradesman, as he guides you through the workings of the Athenian economy.

Welcome, my friends, to the port city of Athens. We have a very strong fleet of ships used for trade and in times of war. Our ships are built of timber from our mountains. They are strong and stable in the waters of the Mediterranean Sea. A typical merchant ship is used for transporting goods to faraway lands and bringing back needed products. This kind of ship is large and round, built for space rather than speed. Our merchant ships travel mainly by sail, but we row them to steer them when necessary. They are quite slow, reaching only about four to six knots. This makes them an easy target for pirates, and it is hard for them to outrun sea storms. Merchants try to sail close to shore and sometimes are accompanied by swifter warships for long journeys that require more protection.

Our warships are built for speed and conquest. They are low to the water and powered by three decks of rowers, who are men in the army. On the front of each ship we paint eyes to watch out for evil spirits and we build a large ramming post to bulldoze into other ships we fight. The success of Athens and other Greek city-states has been because of our ability to control the waters of the Aegean and Mediterranean.

As a trader myself, I have traveled to many islands. We trade mainly in the regions near the Aegean to the east. These include several Greek islands as well as parts of Asia Minor. Some traders have traveled southeast across the Mediterranean as far as Egypt, Assyria, and Phoenecia, and west across the Ionian Sea to trade with parts of the newly formed Roman Empire. Our main exports to these lands include olives and olive oil products, pottery, and metal crafts. Greece is fairly self-sufficient, requiring mostly grain and luxury goods as imports. We are fortunate that we have such a thriving economy!

66

Triton the Trader *(cont.)*

Up until around 600 B.C. we traded using the barter system. This meant that we were able to negotiate trading a certain amount of one type of good for a certain amount of another type of good. Our economy grew rapidly, and we soon became an international trading center. The increased volume of trade required a new system for acquiring goods. The government of each city-state began making gold and silver coins stamped with the symbol of that particular polis. Each coin did not have a fixed rate of exchange, so people bargained with each other until they reached an agreement. Some coins could only be used in their home city-state, while others—like the Athenian coin showing the goddess Athena on one side and the owl, her symbol, on the other—could be used all over the Greek world. This new system using coins allowed the purchase of any product and again spurred on our economy. Now everyone wants to do business with Greece.

I feel fortunate to be a merchant in such a successful polis. As you enter the open market near the Agora you can see the wealth of our city-state. Metics, merchants, and craftsmen all sell their goods alongside food products from our local farms. Farming is still the main source of our economy. Most families have enough land to support their own families, and some wealthy families are able to grow a surplus and sell it for profit. One of the benefits of living in our democracy is the fact that the wealthy families give back to the community rather than hoarding their profits. Each year they donate money to help run the government, beautify and fortify Athens with building projects, help strengthen the naval fleets, and support religious festivals. In this way the wealth is spread throughout the community, and we are able to provide more jobs for more people. Athens truly is a remarkable place to live and work.

Activities

1. Make a map showing the different trade routes used by the Greeks.

2. Draw a picture of the two different types of Greek ships. Label the parts.

3. Make a large Greek coin out of cardboard and foil. Draw a symbol of your city-state on one side using permanent black marker. Use the Greek alphabet to write the name of your polis.

4. Make a chart showing the imports and exports of Greece. Cut pictures out of magazines or draw pictures to accompany your chart.

Count Your Cargo

The Greeks used the letters of their alphabet to also make their numbers. They used 24 letters, plus three additional symbols that are now obsolete. The first nine letters represented numbers 1–9. The next nine letters represented multiples of 10, from 10–90. The last nine letters represented multiples of 100, from 100–900. Counting up to 999 was quite easy if you knew all 27 symbols!

A	alpha	1	I	iota	10	P	rho	100
B	beta	2	K	kappa	20	Σ	sigma	200
Γ	gamma	3	Λ	lambda	30	T	tau	300
Δ	delta	4	M	mu	40	Y	upsilon	400
E	epsilon	5	N	nu	50	Φ	phi	500
	obsolete digamma	6	Ξ	xi	60	X	chi	600
Z	zeta	7	O	omicron	70	Ψ	psi	700
H	eta	8	Π	pi	80	Ω	omega	800
Θ	theta	9		obsolete koppa	90		obsolete sampi	900

To write the numbers, the Greeks combined the letters, starting with the largest value. For example:

NE = 50 + 5 = 55   PKB = 100 + 20 + 2 = 122

Use the chart to write the value of these Greek numbers.

1. TI = _____

2. PNE = _____

3. MΔ = _____

4. ΨΛE = _____

5. TΠΔ = _____

6. OΘ = _____

7. ΦΘ = _____

8. YKA = _____

9. XΞ = _____

Use the chart to write the Greek equivalent of these numbers.

1. 37 = _____

2. 88 = _____

3. 71 = _____

4. 63 = _____

5. 221 = _____

6. 734 = _____

7. 582 = _____

8. 459 = _____

9. 104 = _____

Answers—Fold over or cover before reproducing for students.

1. 310
2. 155
3. 44
4. 735
5. 384

6. 79
7. 509
8. 421
9. 660

1. ΛZ
2. ΠH
3. OA
4. ΞΓ
5. ΣKA

6. ΨΛΔ
7. ΦΠB
8. YNΘ
9. PΔ

Cargo Calculations

One problem with using the same symbols to represent letters and numbers was that some numbers also spelled words, making calculations very confusing indeed. This also led to some superstitions about certain numbers that formed certain words or initials. Write the following Greek numbers to see for yourself.

1. 77 =   3. 370 =   5. 315 =

2. 45 =   4. 115 =   6. 375 =

Use the < or > symbol to compare these Greek numbers. Place it in the O.

7. IB O Λ   10. ΣM O ΣΙΓ   13. ΩK O ΩNΓ

8. ΩΠ O XΠH   11. YN O PA   14. ΠH O OZ

9. NE O NH   12. X O YΞΘ   15. PA O IZ

Add, subtract, multiply, or divide the following Greek numbers. Hint: Write our equivalent first.

16. MΔ + XΞZ = _____   21. (T + MΔ) − PB = _____

17. PIH + YNΘ = _____   22. ΠZ x PKB = _____

18. (ΩN + TKZ) + ΞΘ = _____   23. ΨNE x TMΘ = _____

19. ΦE − TΠH = _____   24. ΩNE ÷ E = _____

20. ΩΞA − ΣKΓ = _____   25. ΦΠH ÷ IΔ = _____

Solve the following Greek story problems.

26. Zamos had a ship full of cargo. He had ME kilos of olives, TB kilos of grapes, XNH kilos of bronze weapons, and PA kilos of pottery. How many total kilos of cargo did Zamos have on his ship?

27. King Misha had XOH gold crowns and KB queens. How many gold crowns could he give to each queen?

28. The Spartans needed bronze shields for their next battle. If they had NZ shield makers that could make POH shields each, how many bronze shields could be made for the battle?

Answers—Fold up or cover before reproducing for students.

1. OZ	7. <	13. <	19. 117	25. 42
2. ME	8. >	14. >	20. 638	26. 1,106
3. TO	9. <	15. >	21. 242	27. 30 R 18
4. PIE	10. >	16. 711	22. 10,614	28. 10,146
5. TIE	11. >	17. 577	23. 263,495	
6. TOE	12. >	18. 1,246	24. 171	

Pi

In order to bargain and trade, the ancient Greeks needed to be able to measure the objects in their environment regardless of their shape and size. Their investigations helped unlock the secrets of the branch of mathematics called geometry (geo = earth, metria = measure). Work in partners to learn how *pi* came to be important to Greek traders.

1. Gather five flat, circular objects of different sizes (plastic lids, jar tops, coins, etc.), a flexible measuring tape, and a calculator.

2. Measure each object's circumference, or the distance around the outside, and record it in decimal form on the chart below.

3. Measure each object's diameter, or distance from one side to the other through the midpoint, and record it in decimal form on the chart.

Circle #	Circumference	Diameter	Ratio C:d, or C/d	Divide	Round to Hundredths
Example	56.5	18	56.5:18, $\frac{56.5}{18}$	3.13888	3.14
1.					
2.					
3.					
4.					
5.					

4. On the chart write the ratio of circumference to diameter, $\frac{C}{d}$ or C:d.

5. Using the calculator, divide each object's circumference by its diameter and record that decimal number on the chart.

6. Round these numbers to the nearest hundredth and record them on the chart.

7. What do you discover about the ratio of circumference to diameter of any circle? _____

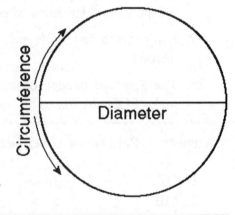

8. After rounding your decimals to hundredth, you should have come up with answers very close to 3.14 for all the circles. This number—3.14—is known as *pi* and is usually written as π. It is used in geometry to make calculations necessary to measure anything that incorporates a circle or part of a circle. What objects of containers having circles might have been measured by Greek traders?

Calculate a Ship's Cargo

Have students experiment with different cargoes to understand the problems facing boat captains when they calculate how much their ship can transport.

Preparing for the lesson:

1. Gather five identical, empty, clean juice cans. Fill each can to the top with one of the following items: cereal, flour, rice, oats, or beans. Tape the tops securely so the material cannot fall out. Clearly label each can with the name of the "cargo" it contains.

2. Gather five of each of the following: scales and sets of weights, calculators, and metric tape measures.

3. Reproduce five Cargo Calculation Charts (page 72).

Teaching the Lesson:

1. Divide the class into five "ship crews." Tell the groups that they have a ship whose maximum cargo volume is 5,000 cc (cubic centimeters) and whose maximum cargo weight is 5,000 g (grams). They will have different types of cargo available for their ship to carry, and they will determine how much of each type of cargo they can transport.

2. Lead the class in a discussion of the relationship of weight to volume. (As the volume [mass] of any one material increases, so does its weight.) If a load is based on weight, the ship can only carry a maximum weight, no matter how much space the cargo material takes up. If a load is based on volume, it can only hold a maximum volume, no matter how much the cargo material weighs.

2. Elicit from students that no matter how much space (volume) a ship may have for cargo, it can still safely carry only the maximum weight—or the ship will sink. In this case, maximum weight is 5,000 g.

3. Give a Cargo Calculation Chart to each group. Display the cargo cans, and choose one to use as an example. Write the necessary formulas on the chalkboard for students to use.

   $V = A \times h$ The volume of a cylinder is calculated by multiplying the area of its base (circle) times its height.

   $A = \pi r^2$ To find the area of the base (circle), you multiply pi (3.14) times the radius squared ($r \times r$).

   $r = \dfrac{d}{2}$ The radius of a circle is $\frac{1}{2}$ its diameter.

4. Find the volume of your sample can. Record it on the Cargo Calculation Chart. If you have identical cans, the volume will be the same for each can.

5. Give each group a can. Have them weigh it and record the result on the chart. Have groups trade cans until each group has weighed all the cans and recorded their weights.

6. Have each group use a calculator to determine how many cans of each cargo the ship can carry: (a) by weight and (b) by volume.

7. Challenge groups to figure out how they can choose their cargo to fill the ship's carrying space yet not exceed its carrying weight. Share and discuss findings together as a class.

Cargo Calculation Chart

Your Greek ship can carry 5,000 cc and 5,000 g of cargo. Complete the chart. Calculate the maximum number of cans of cargo your ship can carry by weight and by volume.

	Weight	Volume	Number of cans by weight (g)	Number of cans by volume (cc)
Cereal				
Flour				
Rice				
Oats				
Beans				

Formulas:

radius = $\frac{1}{2}$ x diameter

Area = pi x r x r, or (3.14 x r2), or πr^2

Volume = Area x height

Which cargo would you carry if you were being paid by the can? _____

Which cargo would you carry if you were being paid by total weight? _____

Travel Log of Trade Routes

Pretend that you are a Greek merchant trading with other lands. Use the scale on the map to find the distance between the various locations. Choose the shortest route. Write in your travel log exactly how you would travel from one location to another. Make sure you include the directions of travel, the distance between one landform to the next, and whether you travel by land or water. Use a different color for each voyage described and trace your routes on the map.

1. Begin at the island of Corfu on the west coast of Greece and travel to Troy in Asia Minor.

2. Leave Troy and go to Knossos on the island of Crete.

3. Take your goods and return home to Corfu.

4. Which route was the longest?

5. Which route required travel over land and sea?

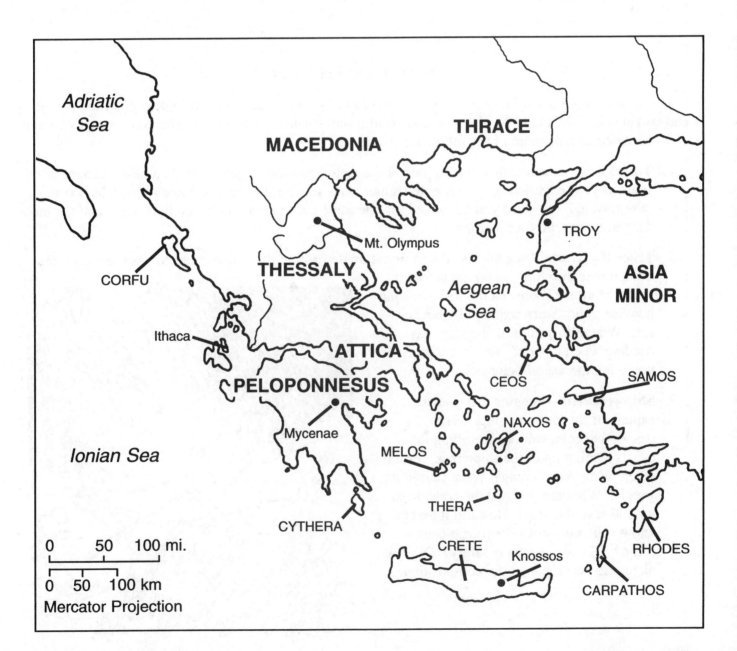

Excavating a Sunken Ship

In 1982 a diver was searching for natural sponges off of the Turkish coastline in an area known as Ulu Burun. Instead he found a treasure of copper ingots! He reported his find to the authorities. A team of archaeologists excavated the site and found the earliest shipwreck ever discovered. A trading vessel from the 14th century B.C. was discovered 150 feet beneath the surface. Still on board were thousands of valuable and historical items. They figured the ship must have sailed the waters of the Mediterranean Sea about the same time as the fall of Troy, when the Mycenaean civilization was flourishing in Greece.

The ship's country of origin is still unknown. From various items found, scientists believe that the crew was most likely a mix of many cultures. The remains of the ship itself do not give many clues about the design of the vessel. Evidence suggests that it was a round-hulled ship about 50 feet long, powered by both sails and oars. This was typical of most merchant vessels designed to carry large quantities of cargo.

Shipwreck Activities

The treasures found aboard the shipwrecked vessel have provided an in-depth look at this time period and taught scientists and historians new and exciting information. Use the information on pages 75 and 76 to complete one or more of the following activities:

1. **Travel Log**—Imagine that you are one of the sailors aboard the ship. Write a brief account of some of your experiences. Be sure to include who you are, where you came from, where you have traveled, the items you bargained for, the most fascinating sights you have seen, and the most dangerous part of your journey.

2. **Trace the Trade Routes**—Use the information describing the ship's cargo to work out possible trade routes the ship was taking before it sank. Mark the routes on the map showing how the goods were acquired by land or by sea. Where do you think the ship was heading when it sank? To what country do you think the vessel belongs?

3. **Shipwrecked!**—Imagine that you are the captain of this doomed ship. Write a descriptive composition describing the events leading up to the shipwreck. From where were you coming? What caused the wreck? What did you and the crew do to try and save the ship? How did it feel to know you could not save your precious cargo? Did you get away safely? Draw a picture to accompany your composition.

Items Excavated from the Shipwreck

- Many of the jars aboard the ship showed Canaanite craftsmanship.

- Most of the jewelry found was of Canaanite design.

- The distinctive pottery of the Mycenaeans was found among the wreckage.

- The original source of many items was traced to areas hundreds of miles away from the Mediterranean Sea coastline.

- The ship contained several stone anchors. Similar types of anchors have been found during earlier excavations near Cyprus, Egypt, and Syria.

- Some amber, a precious gem made from tree sap, was retrieved from the wreck. It has been identified as "Baltic Amber," the type found in Northern Europe.

- Bronze weapons and tools have been recovered which seem to include Mycenaean, Canaanite, and Egyptian workmanship.

- A solid, gold scarab, the sacred beetle in Egypt, was recovered. It bears hieroglyphics that spell the name of Nefertiti, queen of Egypt.

- An enormous storage jar held several smaller items of pottery. Many of the pots were still whole. Scientists were able to identify them as being made in Cyprus during the Bronze Age.

- A tiny rectangular plaque of greenish stone was found with an inscription in Egyptian hieroglyphics that read, "Ptah, Lord of Truth." Ptah was the patron god of craftsmen and was considered by Egyptians to be the creator of the universe.

- Also found was a tremendous amount of jewelry made from gold, silver, and other precious metals. All were in one particular area and all seemed to have been deliberately damaged. Scientists think that perhaps this was a cargo of valuable scrap metal that was going to be melted down and reused.

- The main cargo of the ship was copper ingots, almost 200 in all. Each ingot weighed about 60 pounds. This was consistent with the standard weight measurement of a "talent." One talent was equivalent to about 60 pounds. Archaeologists found this quite intriguing since earlier excavations in Tel el Armarna, the capital of Egypt during the reign of Pharaoh Akhenaten, had revealed clay tablets that described an expected shipment of 200 talents of copper from the king of Cyprus. Were these ingots the promised gift to a pharaoh of Egypt? Could this have been the ship carrying them from Cyprus to Egypt?

- Wood similar to ebony was also found in the shipwreck. This wood was grown in Nubia, an area in Africa south of Egypt. It was the same kind of wood used to make some of the furniture found in King Tutankhamen's tomb in Egypt.

Map of the Shipwreck Area

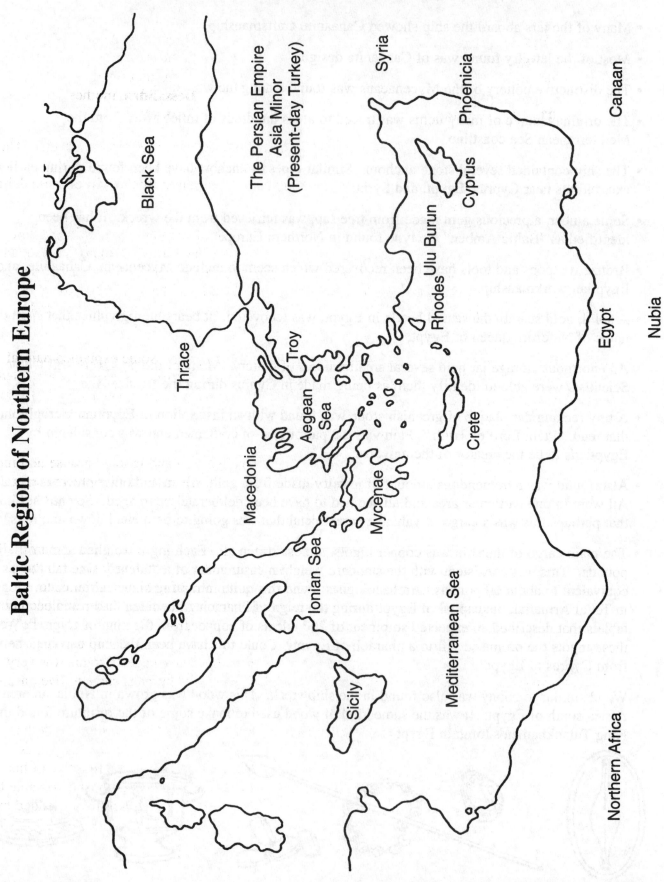

Baltic Region of Northern Europe

Black Sea

The Persian Empire
Asia Minor
(Present-day Turkey)

Syria

Phoenicia

Canaan

Cyprus

Ulu Burun

Rhodes

Egypt

Nubia

Thrace

Troy

Aegean
Sea

Macedonia

Crete

Mycenae

Ionian Sea

Mediterranean Sea

Sicily

Northern Africa

Parsone the Priest

Narrators 1–8
Parsone, Hephest, and **Zeneph,** priests
Cassander, Harpen, and **Stynia,**
priestesses
Sophles, funeral priest
Thestian, brother

Usura, daughter
Dagmared, father
Galatia, sister
Nadina, wife
Dessandra, mother
Trident, son

Narrator 1: Ordinary life and religion were closely related in the world of the Ancient Greeks. The Greeks practiced **polytheism,** or the worship of many gods and goddesses. They believed that everything that happened to them in their lives—good and bad—was caused by the will of these deities. Therefore, everything was personified as a god.

Narrator 2: The Greeks imagined their gods to be superhumanlike in form but also imperfect and lacking total power over the lives of human begins. The Greek gods had human weaknesses, too, and often lost their self-control and showed love, hate, jealousy, anger, and revenge. Worshippers tried to keep the gods happy to ensure their own future good fortune and success. They offered up prayers, **animal sacrifices,** and agricultural products at temples; consulted oracles; and held sporting and dramatic festivals in honor of certain gods.

Narrator 3: They also wrote many **myths** about the activities of the gods. Some explained natural occurrences and some told of how the gods used mortals to create great heroes. These tales are filled with adventure, intrigue, and an impressive array of imaginative creatures, both good and evil. Parsone is a priest at one of the many Greek temples. He and his friends will tell you more about their fascinating religion.

Parsone: Long ago, Gaea, the Earth, came out of darkness. She was sad and lonely because nothing yet lived on her. Above her rose Uranus, the Sky. He was dark and blue with dazzling bright stars. Soon the Earth and Sky fell in love. Gaea became Mother Earth, the mother of all things, and her children loved her dearly, but they feared their mighty father, Lord of the Universe.

Hephest: The Titans were the first gods and children of Mother Earth. They were mighty giants taller than the mountains. Uranus was not pleased with all of his Titan children, so he sent some to the Underworld. This greatly displeased Mother Earth, who convinced one of her sons, Cronus, to overthrow Uranus and release the other Titans. Cronus obeyed, striking down his father and becoming Lord of the Universe. Cronus ruled the heavens and Earth with a firm hand. During his reign, he grew tired of the same company. So he had another Titan create a new creature that was neither bird nor animal nor god. With clay the sculptor modeled a tiny creature in his own image. Cronus was very pleased with this new creature and many more were formed. This is how humans came to live on Earth.

Zeneph: However, Cronus never did free his other Titan brothers from the Underworld, so Mother Earth plotted his downfall. She knew that one of Cronus's sons would be stronger than he, just as Cronus had been stronger than his father. Cronus feared this fate and swallowed the first five of his offspring. One day, his wife, Rhea, gave birth to Zeus. With help from Mother Earth, she was able to deceive her husband and spirit Zeus safely away to a secret cave. There he grew up strong, tended by gentle nymphs and a fairy goat.

Parsone the Priest *(cont.)*

Stynia: The first wife of Zeus was able to trick Cronus into eating a magic herb that made him vomit up the five children he had swallowed. These five children became powerful gods: Poseidon, the God of the Sea; Hades, the God of the Underworld; Hera, the Queen of the Gods; Hestia, the Goddess of the Hearth; and Demeter, the Goddess of the Harvest. With the help of his freed brother and sisters, Zeus was able to overthrow Cronus.

Harpen: Zeus was now Lord of the Universe. But he did not want to rule alone, so he shared his powers with his brothers and sisters. Soon the other Titans and their children revolted, refusing to be ruled by the new gods. Zeus freed the entrapped Titans from the Underworld as his mother had asked years before. They fought fiercely for Zeus and made special weapons for him and his brothers—a trident for Poseidon that could shake the ground and create great waves on the sea, a cap of invisibility for Hades so he could strike his enemies unseen, and mighty lightning bolts for Zeus.

Cassander: Zeus soon won the battle over the Titans and locked them all in the Underworld. But once again Mother Earth became angry at Zeus for sending her children away and tried to punish Zeus with terrible monsters. Zeus won the battles and Mother Earth finally gave up her struggle. A palace was built for the gods atop **Mount Olympus**, the highest mountain in Greece. It was hidden by clouds, prohibiting anyone from entering. In the gleaming hall where light never fails, the **Olympian** gods now sit on 12 golden thrones and reign over heaven and earth. Zeus shares his powers with his five brothers and sisters as well as eight of his children. Hestia chose not to sit on a throne, but instead tends the sacred fire in the hall. And Hades, Zeus's gloomy brother, chose to dwell in his palace in the Underworld, where he rules over the dead.

The Gods on Mount Olympus

Parsone the Priest *(cont.)*

Parsone: The gods themselves are immortal. They live atop Mount Olympus overseeing life on Earth as they feast on sweet ambrosia and drink nectar. Sometimes they visit us in the shape of animals and sometimes as humans. It is true that the gods also make mistakes, but we learn from their mistakes and try to avoid making the same ones ourselves. And since the gods are not responsible for showing us the difference between right and wrong, we do not pray to them for goodness, patience, and understanding. Instead we make offerings to help us gain control over our own lives. Although it is a terrible crime to think of oneself as better than the gods, we do consider ourselves almost equal to them.

Zeneph: Come visit the temple where we work. All temples in Greece look very similar. Every polis has a patron god or goddess who is their protector. Near the Agora a temple is erected to honor and worship this patron god and to serve as its earthly home. For example, the Parthenon in Athens is a grand temple dedicated to Athena, the Goddess of War, Wisdom, Arts, and Crafts.

Hephest: Each temple has a main room, or cella, where a statue of the god is kept. Behind that room is a smaller room where our sacred vessels and robes are stored. There is an outer row of columns around the whole building, and a stone altar is placed in front of the entrance to the cella. Decorations include sculpted friezes and statues painted in bright colors.

Narrator 4: Many of the ancient temples, such as the Parthenon, still stand today as a tribute to Greek craftsmanship. However, many of the walls have crumbled and the brightly colored paint has faded away, showing only the white marble and stone beneath.

Stynia: Our temples are designed to be viewed from the outside only. We have such respect for our gods that we do not enter the temple itself. Instead, we worship at the entrance, where we keep a sacred fire always burning. Here we present offerings and perform rituals such as animal sacrifices at the altar. As priests and priestesses, it is our duty to make sure that the gods are properly worshipped and that their temples and other sacred places are kept orderly.

Narrator 4: Priests and priestesses in Ancient Greece were not formally ordained as in other cultures. They were ordinary officials who took their instructions from higher government officials. Their job was often handed down within the family from one generation to another. Since priesthood was viewed as just another civic duty of a citizen, few priests ever became very powerful. Decisions regarding religion were usually made by the government through magistrates or the people's assembly.

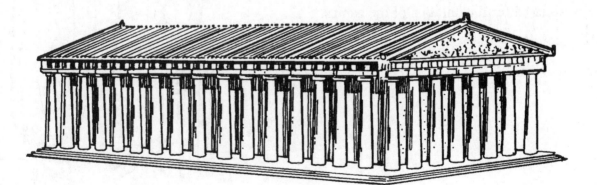

Parsone the Priest *(cont.)*

Narrator 5: The Greeks believed that there were many unseen forces—called *moira*, or fate—at work controlling their lives. Therefore, besides worshipping at the temples they also used every means possible to find out beforehand what the future might hold for them. They consulted priests for interpreting dreams, reading the stars, examining the flight patterns of birds, and examining the entrails of animals. They also consulted **oracles** or soothsayers, who were believed to foretell the future by directly speaking to the gods.

Narrator 6: Since the Greeks believed that females were more intuitive than males, most commonly it was the priestesses who were trained to consult the gods through the medium of trance. Becoming a priestesses or oracle was the only job women were allowed to have. Dagmared and his family have traveled to Delphi to have the famous priestess Pythia consult with the god Apollo.

Dagmared: An oracle can be the sacred place where the gods are consulted, the person in a trance consulting with the gods, or the message from the gods themselves. Public oracles have been established all over Greece, some at temples and some at sacred places such as this in Delphi, where natural gases flow from a hollow in the earth. Soon Pythia will take her high seat on a tripod in the grove of olive trees in a gaseous region. Here she will inhale the vapors, chew narcotic laurel leaves, and then fall into a deep trance and have delirious convulsions.

Dessandra: Nearby a priest awaits to interpret and translate her incoherent words from Apollo himself. We travel with many others on this seventh day of each month to hear the prophecy. We hope that these words of wisdom will help guide our actions in the future. Although we are just ordinary citizens, kings and leaders of armies also consult the oracles.

Thestian: I enjoy coming to hear the oracles, but I prefer the many religious festivals held to worship the gods. Since physical training is important to us, our festivals always feature various athletic events, as well as processions, rites, and rituals. The famous competitive games held every four years at Olympia are dedicated to the god Zeus. The **Olympics** are panhellenic games, which means that all Greeks from across the Mediterranean region are allowed to take part. For this special occasion, heralds are sent throughout the Greek world and truce is declared for the duration of the games.

Parsone the Priest *(cont.)*

Galatia: We have many other festivals to celebrate the harvest and spring and to worship various gods. In Athens there are about 150 festivals each year. One of my favorites is the Festival of Dionysus, held in the spring. Dionysus is the God of Wine, Theater, and Fertility. People travel from all over to join in the celebration and view the famous drama competition at the theater. Our family attends the **theater** throughout the year to learn about and worship the gods, much like you and your family might go to a temple or church. During the Festival of Dionysus the plays go on for days, and prizes are awarded to the playwrights.

Narrator 7: The Greeks had many joyous celebrations to worship their gods. This showed they liked to live life to the fullest. Another important feature of their religion was their belief in the soul. They made elaborate preparations of a deceased relative for his or her journey to the Underworld, an underground kingdom called **Tartarus** ruled by Hades and the final resting place for all mortals.

Trident: My father has recently passed on, and the family is now preparing for the funeral. His body has been washed and anointed with sweet-smelling olive oils. A coin was placed under his tongue to pay his fare into the Underworld. The women of the family dressed him in clean white robes, and he has been put on display for all of our friends and relatives to view. In this way, we each have a chance to pay our last respects to an honored man.

Usura: Tomorrow, before the sun is up, the funeral procession will set out to accompany the body to the burial site. Only our closest relatives will take part. However, any women over 60 are allowed to join in as professional mourners, beating their chests and wailing. The body will be carried on a horse-drawn cart while music plays.

Nadina: The tomb of my husband is very important to ensure his soul is not lost forever. In some cases, death is sudden and three handfuls of dirt are thrown over the body to keep the soul from wandering. Food, drink, and treasured objects used by my husband will be left inside his tomb. After the funeral, our family will return home for a special dinner. We will continue mourning for at least 30 days.

Sophles: Once rested in the tomb, the soul makes its journey to **Tartarus**, which begins at the River Styx. The soul uses the coin under its tongue to pay Charon, who rows the ferryboat to the other side of the river. Souls who cannot pay the fare have to wait on this side of the river. Sometimes these souls come back to haunt those who did not give them the fare!

Parsone the Priest (cont.)

Trident: Once Charon rows across the River Styx, the soul is let off at a great wall. Its gate is guarded by Cerberus, a three-headed dog with an appetite for live meat. He attacks anyone who is not a spirit. Beyond this gate is a great, wide, tree-shaded field where the dead await trial. Those who have greatly displeased the gods are given special punishments. For example, an evil king was given the task of pushing a great boulder uphill forever, never to reach the top. Another evil man was given a burning thirst and placed neck high in water. Every time he bends to get a drink, the water shrinks away, so that he will be thirsty for eternity.

Usura: Most souls are judged as not too good and not too bad. They go back to the field behind the gates to wander forever. This field is called the Field of Asphodel. Some souls are judged to have unusual virtue. They go to the glorious **Elysian Fields**, where the air is filled with sweet music and the spirits dance and play all day and night. These happy souls have the option of being reborn on Earth.

Nadina: There is also a special part of the Elysian Fields called the Isles of the Blest. Here live those souls who have chosen to be reborn three times and each time have earned their way into the Elysian fields. This is the grandest and most joyous part of Tartarus.

Sophles: Hades, the God of the Underworld, Death, and Greed, and his queen live in a great palace made from black rock. He is very jealous of his brothers and rarely leaves his kingdom. He is fiercely possessive and demands a head count from Charon each day. He never allows any spirit to leave Tartarus, nor any mortal to enter.

Trident: The palace grounds of Hades are in the deepest part of the Underworld. No birds fly here, but you can hear the wingbeats of the furies. These are three women older than the gods, with snaky hair, red-hot eyes, and yellow teeth. They slash the air with metal-studded whips, and when they find a victim, they whip him to the bone. Their task is to visit Earth and punish evil-doers. They are greatly feared in Greece, as are their monstrous relatives. We can only hope that our father is judged well and that he will wander in the Field of Asphodel or possibly gain entrance to the Elysian Fields.

Narrator 8: While other cultures lived in fear of cruel and unexplainable gods, the Greeks were fearless. They believed that they needed only to worship their gods to gain more control over their lives. The many myths about the exploits of the gods and their counterparts helped the Greeks to better understand the world around them and learn important lessons to build character important to Greek culture such as bravery, beauty, and humility.

Parsone the Priest—Vocabulary and Comprehension

The following words from the story can be used by students in their Vocabulary Journals (page 5). Remind students to write a complete definition of each word and illustrate them if they wish.

polytheism	**Olympians**	**Olympics**
myths	**animal sacrifices**	**theater**
Mount Olympus	**oracles**	**Tartarus**
		Elysian Fields

All or some of the following questions can be used for whole class discussion, small group work, or individual assessment. Allow students to refer back to the passage while working.

1. How did the Greeks explain the creation of man? How is this similar or different to your own beliefs? *(A Titan formed man in his own image out of clay. Answers will vary depending on beliefs.)*

2. Where do the Olympians live? How is this similar to the concept of God in heaven? *(On Mount Olympus where they are high in the clouds and can view what goes on below. This is similar to God being up in heaven and looking down on Earth.)*

3. In what ways did the Ancient Greeks worship and consult with their gods? *(They gave offerings and sacrifices at temples, they held religious festivals such as the Olympics and drama festivals to Dionysus, and they consulted the gods at oracles to foretell the future.)*

4. Why was it unusual for this culture to have a woman be a priest or oracle? Why then did they allow it? *(Women were not allowed to take part in public life or have jobs, but the Greeks believed women to be more intuitive and therefore best suited to talk with the gods.)*

5. How was a Greek funeral similar to a funeral today? *(The body was cleaned and dressed in fine clothes. Some people still have the body viewed before it is buried. The body is buried in a tomb.)*

6. The Greeks had Tartarus, or Underworld, which represented the resting place for souls. What parts of Tartarus are similar to the modern concept of heaven and hell? Who might Hades represent? *(The punishments were similar to those who go to hell after they die. The Elysian Fields and Isles of the Blest are comparable to heaven. Hades would be the Greek form of the devil. Note: In modern times the word "Hades" actually has become synonymous for the place "hell.")*

7. The Greek gods were unusual in that they had many weaknesses and did not always act in the most perfect way. Why then did the Greeks worship these gods? *(The Greeks did not look at the gods as role models for perfect behavior. They did believe that the gods had a hand in what happened around them. They shared myths about the gods to better explain the world around them and learned from the gods' mistakes to build character. The Greeks gave offerings to the gods and consulted oracles so that they would have more control over their lives.)*

Identify the Greek Gods

Have your students research the Greek gods and create informative and colorful posters.

Preparing for the lesson:

1. Gather 14 large white poster boards, sheets of drawing paper, or sheets of white butcher paper, as well as drawing materials such as crayons, markers, and colored pencils.

2. Gather books and other research materials showing pictures and describing the different Greek gods. You may want to have students go to local libraries to find additional books for their group to use. Good sources include: *D'Aulaires' Book of Greek Myths* by Ingri and Edgar Parin D'Aulaire (Doubleday), *The Olympians, Great Gods and Goddesses of Ancient Greece* by Leonard Everett Fisher (Holiday House), *Favorite Greek Myths* by Mary Pope Osborne (Scholastic), and *The Greek Gods* by Evslin, Evslin, and Hoopes (Scholastic).

3. Reproduce a copy of The Greek Gods (page 85) for each student.

4. Draw a template of a poster on the board or on a large sheet of paper showing the six sections and their labels as shown below.

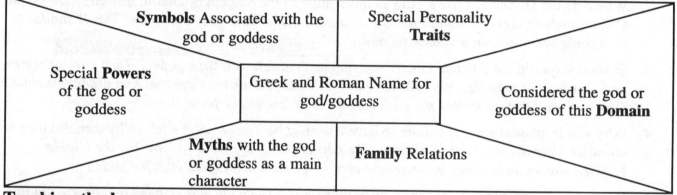

Teaching the lesson:

1. Divide the class into 14 groups and assign each group a work area and one of the 14 Olympians: Zeus, Hades, Poseidon, Hestia, Hera, Demeter, Ares, Hephestus, Athena, Apollo, Artemis, Aphrodite, Hermes, or Dionysus.

2. Distribute the poster board, drawing materials, and research materials. Have each group replicate the template you drew.

3. Have students put shortened headings in the outer sections according to your sample labeled template: Symbols, Traits, Powers, Myths, Family, Domain. Review with them the information that should be recorded in each section. Remind students that they may find information under the Roman name for their god as well.

4. Distribute and review with students how to read The Greek Gods chart. The Greek name is given first; the Roman name is in parentheses; the domain is next, followed by the symbol or symbols and a description that may encompass powers, domain, or traits. Tell students this is a starting point, but to make their posters complete they will have to do more research.

5. Have them fill the center section with their god's name in Greek and Roman.

6. Have students research and record information on their gods. Encourage them to illustrate and decorate their posters to make them more interesting and colorful.

7. Share the posters and display them around the room.

The Greek Gods

Uranus (Heaven) + Gaea (Earth)

⬇

The Titans
(including Cronus and Rhea)

(Roman names appear in parenthesis)

⬇

The Olympians

Hestia	Poseidon	Zeus	Hera	Hades	Demeter
(Vesta) Goddess of the Hearth *Fire* Protector of home and family	(Neptune) God of the Seas (and sea travel) *Trident, horse, bull* Gave the horse to man	(Jupiter) King of the Gods *Eagle, shield, thunderbolt, oak tree* Ruled weather, skies, Mount Olympus	(Juno) Queen of the Gods (wife of Zeus) *Peacock, cow* Protector of marriage; very jealous	(Pluto) God of the Dead and Underworld God of Wealth and Greed *Helmet, metals, jewels*	(Ceres) Goddess of the Harvest and Growth *Grain* Mother of Persephone, who guides the seasons

⬇

Ares	Hephestus
(Mars) God of War and Violence *Vulture, dog* Unliked by all	(Vulcan) God of the Forge (Blacksmith) *Fire, blacksmith hammer* Born with deformed foot Maker of armor and weapons Married to Aphrodite

Olympian Children of Zeus and Others

Athena	Apollo	Artemis	Aphrodite	Hermes	Dionysus
(Minerva) Goddess of Wisdom, War, Arts and Crafts *Owl, olive branch* Sprang from head of Zeus (no mother) Protector of Athens Created olive tree, ship, plow Taught cooking, sewing, weaving	(Apollo) God of Light, Truth, Healing, Archery, Music *Crow, dolphin, laurel tree, lyre* Handsome, talented, charming Most loved of all the gods	(Diana) Goddess of the Hunt and Moon *Stag, moon, cypress tree* Twin to Apollo Protector of children and young animals	(Venus) Goddess of Love and Beauty *Dove, sparrow, swan, myrtle tree* Born out of the foamy sea (no mother) Her son Eros (Cupid) caused people to fall in love	(Mercury) God of Sleep and Dreams *Winged helmet, sandals, wand from Apollo* Messenger of Zeus Protector of Travelers Led the dead to Underworld	(Bacchus) God of Wine and Fertility *Grapes, wine, theater masks* Born to a mortal Worshipped with drama festivals

Religion

Draw and Describe the Greek Gods

Have students enjoy an art and poetry project in which they can bring their favorite gods to "life."

Preparing for the lesson:

1. Cut eight sheets of white butcher paper and eight sheets of black butcher paper about the size of a large child.

2. Assemble pictures of the gods, sets of colored chalks or pastels, glue, scissors, and two cans of inexpensive hair spray to "set" the chalk.

3. Gather writing materials and resources such as dictionaries and thesauruses.

4. Divide the class into eight groups and have each group choose a god to write a poem about and draw.

Teaching the poetry lesson:

1. Distribute the writing materials to each group. Have groups divide their papers into four sections labeled: God of—, Looks, Personality, and Famous for—.

2. Have groups brainstorm information for each section using available reference materials.

3. Tell groups to write their poems (rhyming or free verse) using a variety of descriptive language such as similes, metaphors, and personification to describe their god. Example:

POSEIDON, GUARDIAN AND MASTER OF THE SAPPHIRE WATERS;
PRODUCER AND CONTROLLER OF THE
RIPPLING WAVES.
RADIANT, TALL, AND VIGOROUS, LIKE THE
POWERFUL BLUE WHALE,
A STERN EXPRESSION ON HIS BEARDED FACE.
HANDSOME AND LOVED BY THETIS AND
AMPHITITRITE;
HEART-BREAKER OF THE SEA NYMPHS.
HIS RAGING TEMPER CAUSES THE EARTH
ABOVE
TO TREMBLE AND SHAKE.
BUILDER OF UNDERSEA WORLDS;
RULER OF SEAFARERS' AND TRADERS'
JOURNEYS ACROSS THE SEA.
TRANSFORMED HIMSELF INTO A GREAT STALLION FOR DEMETER;
GIFT-GIVER OF THE HORSE FOR MAN TO FOREVER ENJOY.

4. Circulate around the room to provide help if needed. Share good examples with the class to provide them ideas for using descriptive language.

5. Have groups type or neatly write final drafts of their poems. Display the poems next to the gods on a bulletin board, or glue them onto the back of the gods and suspend them from the ceiling.

Draw and Describe the Greek Gods *(cont.)*

Teaching the art lesson:

1. Trace around a large student on the white butcher paper in a pose appropriate for the god/goddess. Clean-up the lines by drawing in the appropriate proportions of feet, hands, face, etc., so that students have good guide lines to follow.

2. Have students use colored chalks or pastels to draw in the features of the god/goddess. Circulate around the room to offer help if needed. Show students how to shade the drapery of the costumes and draw well-proportioned faces.

3. The students may wish to have the god/goddess hold something that is one of their symbols. For example: Athena might hold a shield with an owl on it, Zeus might hold a lightning bolt, Poseidon a trident, Hades a skull, Apollo his lyre, Hermes his winged helmet and sandals, etc.

4. Once the life-size god is completed, have groups outline in brown the facial features and other skin areas to help make the features stand out. If necessary, also have groups outline their god/goddess's costume in a darker color to accentuate the folds and other features.

5. While students are out of the room, spray the chalk drawings with at least two coats of hairspray held about 12 inches (30 cm) away from the drawing. This will help keep the chalk from rubbing off.

6. Cut out the god/goddess and glue it onto the black sheet of butcher paper. (This will require more than one person). Cut out the god/goddess again, leaving about one inch (3 cm) of black paper around the edge. Now the life-size god is framed and is sturdy enough to mount on a bulletin board or hang from the ceiling. Label the drawing in black marker with the name of the god/goddess.

Write a Greek Myth

Have students write a myth using the elements of a classical Greek myth.

Preparing for the lesson:

1. Gather books and other resources containing a variety of Greek myths that explain natural phenomena. Good stories to share include those of Persephone, who was stolen by Hades and explains why we have the seasons; Arachne, who challenged Athena to a weaving contest and was ultimately turned into a spider; Echo, who was punished by the jealous Hera and made to repeat whatever was said to her; Io and how the peacock was given eyes on its feathers; Dionysus and why dolphins are like humans; Prometheus and how man got fire; and Deucalion and the great flood that covered the earth and how he escaped on an ark.

2. Reproduce the Story Plot Outline (page 47) and Editing Checklist (page 18) for each student.

3. Create an overhead transparency of the Story Plot Outline and The Writing Process (page 17).

4. Write the Elements of a Greek Myth on the chalkboard or create a poster for students to refer to while writing.

   A classical Greek myth:
   - explains a natural phenomenon or the creation of something.
   - depicts a struggle between good and evil characters.
   - shows a relationship between mortals and the supernatural.
   - contains magical characters, gods, goddesses, nymphs, giants, etc.
   - sometimes depicts a hero's quest to accomplish a great feat.
   - makes reference to geological places and cultural aspects of Ancient Greece.

Teaching the lesson:

1. Read several Greek myths to the class. You may choose to find a book containing several myths and read a portion each day.

2. Analyze the myths together and discuss common elements found in each one. Display and review the Elements of a Greek Myth above.

3. Tell students that they will write their own Greek myths using these elements. Brainstorm together some subjects for their stories: Why there is rain, rainbows, waves, sunrise, lightning, clouds, phases of the moon, earthquakes, hurricanes, thunder, etc. Why different plants or animals have certain traits, why man does things a certain way, etc.

4. Using the overhead transparencies, review The Writing Process and Story Plot Outline. Distribute the Story Plot Outline pages to students to use for their prewriting stage.

5. Once students have completed their rough drafts, distribute the Editing Checklist pages and review how students should use the page to enhance their composition.

6. Have students complete their final drafts and share them with the class. Evaluate the stories based on the students' use of the Greek myth elements and understanding of story plot sequence.

The Greek Olympics

The Ancient Greeks loved games and competition. The original goal of all athletic games was to produce physical strength, stamina, and skill much needed in daily life and when at war. The Greeks put a high value on health, strength, and physical beauty. Because of this, Greek men and boys went to "work out" at the local gymnasium. Here they practiced wrestling, throwing the javelin and discus, running, jumping, and boxing. Exercising the mind was also considered important, so males discussed ideas, gave advice, and watched other athletes train. The gymnasium was a kind of men's club in which males of any social class could join. Women were excluded.

Originally, individual gymnasiums would conduct competitions in certain athletic events. Around 776 B.C. the Greeks began to hold organized games at the polis of Olympia. These games were held every four years and open to the finest athletes from all over the Greek world. During the games all fighting would cease so that the athletes could train and compete. These first "Olympics" were more than just a sporting contest. The games were held in honor of Zeus because the Greeks believed that the gods were pleased with mortals' application of hard work and personal achievement.

The first Olympics lasted only one day but gradually grew to a full week of competition. As the festival grew in importance, each polis sent athletes who had excelled in their gymnasiums. No points were recorded to gauge how each city-state measured against another. All that mattered was that individual winners came from Sparta, Athens, Phoenicia, or Corinth. Originally, only adult males competed. But by 632 B.C. sporting events for boys ages 17–20 were introduced. Records indicate that no females competed at the Olympics—they had to be satisfied with being spectators. To the Greeks, the human body, clothed or not, was a temple to build and admire, and well-toned athletes were examples of the perfect male body. Therefore, it was not unusual for women and children to be in the audience as athletes competed in the nude.

The Olympic games attracted a cross-section of spectators from around the Greek world. Since there was no cost for attending the games, Greeks from every social class and occupation journeyed to Olympia for the great festival to Zeus. Between sporting events, other exciting attractions entertained the crowds. Tents and booths were set up around the stadium in a carnival-like fashion. Peddlers sold products and services, while orators, philosophers, artists, acrobats, magicians, writers, and even pickpockets circulated through the masses. There were other problems and great inconveniences, such as no drinking water, no toilets, millions of flies, and a hot August sun, but these did not deter people from coming to enjoy the games.

The Greek Olympics *(cont.)*

Most athletes arrived in Olympia at least one month prior to the competitions. During this time they trained physically and were prepared by priests to become pure in thought and deed. Finally, the games would begin.

Day One: The first day of the Olympic Games was spent in religious observance and worship. Each athlete vowed to compete in true sportsmanship. Then animal sacrifices were offered to Zeus near his grand temple.

Day Two: The second day began with chariot races—two-wheeled carts drawn by four horses— followed by an 800-meter bareback horse race. There were a number of footraces, some wrestling and boxing, and horse racing. On this day the boys also competed.

Day Three: This day was devoted to the pentathlon, a grueling test of stamina and skill that had contestants competing in five different events in one day— a 200-meter run, wrestling, long jump, discus throw, and javelin toss. All events except for wrestling were held in the stadium.

Day Four: This final day of competition started with a 200-meter dash. The rest of the day was then devoted to such popular contact sports as wrestling and boxing. Wrestling contests took place in mud and dust. The dust made it easier to get a hold on one's opponent, while the mud made it more difficult. To win, an athlete had to pin his opponent's shoulders to the ground three times, the method still used today. In boxing, athletes wore bronze caps to protect their heads from their opponent's fists, which were armed with leather thongs studded with metal. The final contact event, the pankration, was a combination of wrestling, boxing, and judo. In this bloody event the athletes could punch, kick, and even strangle their opponents until they surrendered. To complete the Olympic Games, athletes wearing full armor competed in a 400-meter race.

Day Five: Usually scheduled to coincide with the full moon, this last day was for celebration and religious observances, culminating in more sacrifices to Zeus. The victors' names would be read aloud before the altar of Zeus. These champions would receive a wreath of olive leaves to wear on their heads. Many won prizes such as olive oil, fine horses, or privileges such as being exempt from paying taxes or being excused from military service. These men returned to their city-states as honored heroes.

For nearly a thousand years the Greeks enjoyed the Olympic Games. But in A.D. 394 a Roman emperor believed that the games had no place in the Christian world and banned them. For the next 1500 years there were no organized athletic events held on the scale of those in Olympia. They were not revived until 1896, when the first "modern" Olympics were held in Athens. Since then, every four years (with only three exceptions) athletes and spectators from around the world have looked forward to, trained for, and enjoyed the Olympic Games.

Estimation Pentathlon

Name _____ Total Score _____

Set up five event stations by taping one or more metric measuring tapes onto the appropriate surfaces and extending appropriate distances. Rotate through each athletic event as a contestant and as a scorekeeper/verifier for other contestants. Before you begin an event, record the distance in centimeters you estimate you will achieve. After your turn at an event, check with the score verifier and record the actual distance you achieved. Ask the verifier to initial the score. Then subtract the two distances, and record that result as your score. At the end of the pentathlon, add up your scores for the five events and record it above for Total Score. Compare your total score with those of your classmates to determine the overall winner and the winner of each event.

Paper Plate Discus Toss a stiff paper plate like a discus (<u>not</u> a frisbee) along the measuring tapes.

Estimate	Actual	Difference/Score

Plastic Straw Javelin Throw a plastic straw like a javelin.

Estimate	Actual	Difference/Score

Cotton Ball Shotput Throw a large ball of cotton like a shotput.

Estimate	Actual	Difference/Score

Standing Broad Jump Jump from behind a starting line; keep both feet together. You may want to swing your arms to help gain distance.

Estimate	Actual	Difference/Score

Spoon/Clay Pole Vault Hold your "vaulting" hand on a chair seat; put a ball of clay into the spoon's bowl, and flip it as high as you can against a wall covered with paper. Have the verifier mark where it hits, then measure.

Estimate	Actual	Difference/Score

Drama Festival to Honor Dionysus

One of the greatest contributions of the Ancient Greeks to Western culture was their invention of drama and the theater. The word "drama" means "to act or do." Like most Greek rituals these dramas were part of religious festivals. By the 6th century B.C. the worship of one deity in particular, Dionysus, the God of Wine and Fertility, became the prominent focus of these drama festivals. Athenians were expected to thank Dionysus for his gifts with celebrations that included dancing, wild music, and speaking.

For years Greek drama did not fit our modern image of theater. In 534 B.C., Thespis, a native of Attica, changed the drama's structure. He added an actor who spoke, in addition to the chorus historically used in plays. "Actor" means "to lead" in Greek. Now there was dialogue on stage, and this opened up possibilities for further changes over the centuries. Modern-day actors call themselves "thespians" after this famous Greek playwright.

By the time of Pericles and the Golden Age of Athens, Greek drama had become the most popular form of entertainment. Ancient Greece produced some of the greatest playwrights in Western civilization. Their masterpieces of tragedy and comedy still touch us today as they did when they were first performed. What Athenians watched and heard in their open-air theaters was more than just entertainment. The plays were usually a lesson in public education and dealt with issues important to Greek people—power, justice, morality, war, and peace, and man's relationship with the gods, family, and the city-state.

Sisyphus and Marsyas two Greek children looked forward to the spring and the Festival to Dionysus, when Athens would become more crowded than ever as visitors came from far and near. The Agora teemed with interesting people from all over the Greek world recounting tales of faraway places and people. The guest rooms of their farmhouse were filled with relatives and guests who had journeyed long just to attend the festival. The highlight of the week would be the drama competition in which plays would continue for four days. Playwrights presented their best works for the judging. Families took a holiday from work and school to enjoy the theater fest.

Each day of the festival the family arose early to prepare for the day-long theater event. Marsyas and her mother baked fresh loaves of bread and packed large containers of food for the day. Sisyphus and his father filled jugs with wine and water to quench their thirst as they sat long hours in the open and sunshine. They also made sure they had plenty of cushions for the family to sit upon, since the wooden seats of the theater were quite hard.

Drama Festival to Honor Dionysus *(cont.)*

The family left the farm for the city before daybreak. When they arrived it was already crowded. They made their way to the Acropolis, where the theater was. The children were excited and looked forward to seeing friends and other relatives there. A block of seats was reserved for each family tribe, so they knew where to go once they entered the great open-air theater. Sisyphus and his family bought tickets that gave them access to the better seats. Athenians too poor to afford tickets were allowed in free. No one was denied access to the theater.

The noise outside the theater was deafening. As friends and family members greeted each other and children ran around excitedly, actors and playwrights tried to convince them to vote for their play. Marsyas always became quite breathless when she entered the theater, and she held tightly to her mother's hand. Rows and rows of wooden seats rose high on both sides of the entrance, creating a tunnel effect.

What a sight they beheld as the audience took their seats and fell silent for the opening procession. Priests entered the theater, carrying a statue of Dionysus. They crossed the floor of the theater. This was the orchestra, or dancing ground. This is where the chorus performed. They walked to an altar in the center of the orchestra. Sacrifices were offered, then the altar was moved up to the stage. Now the plays could begin! A flute player led the chorus of 15 men wearing brightly colored costumes into the orchestra. Throughout the play the chorus chanted, danced, clowned, and interacted with the actors as they told the story. The chorus acted much like modern narrators today. The actors came out onto the stage from a *skene*, a small wooden building that looked like a temple or palace. Most of the action of the drama would take place at the front of the stage.

Many of the great Greek plays are still being performed in theaters like this.

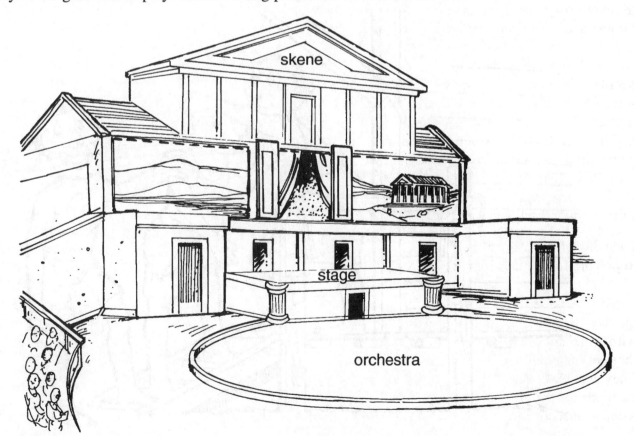

Drama Festival to Honor Dionysus *(cont.)*

Soon the chorus introduced the first play. Sisyphus knew the story well—most plays were about well-known heroes, legends, and myths. What he really looked forward to was how each playwright interpreted the story, how the actors performed their roles, and the special effects used to enhance the production. Sisyphus and Marsyas were wide-eyed as a crane carrying the main actor in a golden chariot made it appear he was were flying through the sky to land on the stage.

In all Greek plays, a handful of male actors played all the roles. Since there was little time to change costumes, actors only changed large masks that showed their emotions, such as fear, hate, love, laughter, and compassion. The actors also wore thick-soled shoes, wigs, and extra padding to alter their shapes and sizes. After the first play was over the audience enjoyed refreshments and waited for the next performance. Children grew sleepy in the heat and often dozed off during the grown-up and more serious sections of the drama. However, everyone tried to be awake for the final performance, a comedy. At the end of this busy day filled with laughter and merriment, families made their way home and travelers went to their lodgings to rest up for the next day of dramas.

The drama competitions usually presented three comedies and three tragedies. Prizes were awarded to the writers of the best tragedy and best comedy. The winning playwrights were crowned with wreaths of olive branches. Going to the theater back then was much like going to the opera or a musical today, with singing and dancing by the chorus in between scenes, but the atmosphere was very different. As with the Olympic Games, this competition was a festive and rowdy event. The audience was almost as interesting to watch as the play itself. They would hiss, groan, shout, and clap to show how they felt about what was happening. Some kicked the benches and seats to show displeasure. In return sometimes actors would throw nuts into the crowd as a bribe for their silence.

Create a Greek Drama

Challenge your class to perform a short drama in Greek style with a chorus and only three actors.

Preparing for the lesson:

1. Divide the class into drama groups with seven or eight students in each group.

2. Choose appropriate material for the dramas, such as a reenactment of a famous Greek myth, a chapter from the Literature Connection (pages 153-174), or an original work written by the drama group. Another good source for short Greek plays is *Mythology I, Overhead Transparencies for Creative Dramatics* (Creative Teaching Press).

Teaching the lesson:

1. Tell the groups that they are going to perform a short Greek drama for the class. They will be evaluated on how well they tell the story and perform authentically with a chorus and actors wearing masks.

2. Assign each group a story to reenact. Discuss possible ways to structure the dramas.

   - The chorus enters and introduces the drama by giving necessary background information in unison speaking, chanting, singing, or dancing.

   - The actors enter and proceed with dialogue, wearing appropriate masks and costumes.

   - Each time a costume/mask change is needed, or when the plot changes scenes, the chorus should enter and describe through singing and dancing what is taking place. The chorus can also interject with sound effects or emphasis during the actors' dialogues.

   - Determine what the lesson is, and stage a climax scene depicting this.

   - The chorus ends the drama by explaining the moral and lessons expressed by the play.

3. Allow time for each group to assign three actors and a chorus. The actors will play all of the roles in the drama, so they will need to plan for simple costumes and mask changes. (See the following lesson on making Greek masks.) The chorus will need to plan simple dance/movements and appropriate messages for speaking in unison/singing to help narrate the action of the drama.

4. Have groups plan and practice their dramas. Sometimes it is easiest for the actors of the group to work separately from the chorus once the actual sequence of the drama has been established.

5. Have students perform their dramas for the class. Evaluate their ability to clearly tell the story and effectively use the chorus and actors. (You may wish to do this again during the section called Living History—A Day in Ancient Greece.)

Make a Greek Mask

Every Greek actor wore a mask while on stage. It was usually made from stiffened linen or cut out of cork. The expression was exaggerated so that the entire audience could see. The mouth was made with a large opening so that the actor could project his voice. When the actors changed parts or needed to show a different feeling, they simply changed masks. Have your students create Greek masks for display or to use in a drama of their own.

Preparing for the lesson:

1. Gather for each student a 9" x 12" (23 cm x 30 cm) sheet of stiff construction paper, colored construction paper scraps, scissors, glue, crayons, and markers.

2. Gather a hole puncher, yarn or elastic, and hole reinforcers.

Teaching the lesson:

1. Have student pairs hold construction paper against their partner's face and carefully mark the position of the eyes, nose, mouth, and chin. Tell them to let the paper extend at least two inches below the chin.

2. Have students decide on an expression for their mask. On the chalkboard, draw an example of the expressions and label them with the emotions they depict. Show students how to draw in the angle of the eyes, eyebrows, and mouth to help convey the expressions.

3. Have students cut out the eyes of the mask, make a wedge cut for the nose, and cut an enlarged mouth hole to allow clear speech. Tell them to round the bottom edge of their mask and cut the rest to a desired shape. Ears, hair, and other features and decorations can be added with other scraps of construction paper and crayons or markers.

4. Demonstrate for students how to cut two parallel slits at the chin of the mask about 1 inch (2 cm) apart from each other and overlap them to contour the mask. Then show them how to glue down the flap on top of the overlap.

5. Help students position their masks on their faces, then punch holes on either side, reinforce them, and add yarn or elastic to hold the masks in place.

Surprise

Anger/Evil

Sad

Happy/Love

Sparta and the Persian War

Narrators 1–5   **Spartacus**, their younger son
Theo, husband and father   **Zeke**, their older son
Deidre, his wife   **Amphra**, their daughter

Narrator 1: Greek political and cultural life was centered in the individual polises. Each polis was intensely nationalistic, its people were devoted patriots, and its location was often isolated from its neighbors. One of the strongest city-states was Sparta, located in the southern part of the Peloponnesus peninsula. Lacking enough land to grow food for all its people, Sparta conquered other lands and created slave labor. By 600 B.C. there were about ten slaves for every Spartan citizen, making the ratio 25,000 citizens to 250,000 slaves.

Narrator 2: The slaves rebelled. Being so outnumbered, it took almost 20 years for the Spartans to regain control. Vowing to never let that happen again, Sparta created a fiercely strong army dominated by harsh lifestyle and vigorous training. Their army was unparalleled and feared by all. Let's join a typical family from Sparta as they tell us about life in their city-state.

Theo: I am proud to be a citizen of Sparta. Our government began with two kings ruling together. Eventually the two kings shared power with a 30-man senate, thereby creating an oligarchy. The members of the senate are elected by the citizen Assembly and are required to be at least 60 years old. The Assembly also elects five government leaders called *ephors*. The senate and the ephors are the only ones who can propose new laws or changes in policy. Although all Spartan males over age 30 belong to the Assembly, our job is only to vote yes or no on the laws and policies presented by the senate and ephors.

Narrator 3: Although the Spartans had an Assembly and elected officials, all power was really in the hands of a few families who dominated the senate and controlled the ephors. Even if the Assembly voted against the senate on a law, the senate and ephors often ignored this vote. A truly democratic government allowing many choices never developed in Sparta. Still, this government did create a very stable and proud society that believed it to be superior to others.

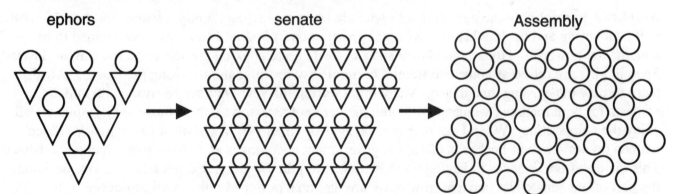

ephors   senate   Assembly

Zeke: I am the son of Theo. At age 18, I am not yet a full citizen. All sons of Spartan citizens are trained as soldiers. The military is the basis for our economy and citizens of Sparta can only work in the military. Work involving trade, craftsmanship, or anything else outside the military are left to noncitizens. These jobs are not important to us because we require few luxury goods. We believe that dependence on items that make life more comfortable only creates a society of weak people. Though we obviously must eat, we also limit our intake of food. The government gives us a plot of land and *helots*, or state slaves, to farm it to provide what food we do require.

Sparta and the Persian War *(cont.)*

Theo: All family life in our city-state is controlled by the government. Husbands and wives do not spend much time together, since husbands are usually off training or fighting battles. By the age of 30, a man gains full citizenship, completes his military training, and is allowed to marry. Even after he is married, he continues to live only in the company of other men.

Deidre: My husband is now 50 and an important leader in the army. Our family has not been together for many years. Zeke has lived at the military barracks for over ten years, and our younger son, Sparticus, joined the army two years ago, when he was seven. Amphra is now 13. She will most likely marry in the next five years and set up a home of her own. Theo and I see each other infrequently. The last time Theo came home was five years ago, when our baby Sophie was born. Since it is important in our society that we bear only healthy and strong babies, government inspectors came with him to decide whether or not Sophie was fit to be a Spartan citizen. If they decide a child is weak or unfit, they will take the baby and put it out to die. Although this seems harsh, we all believe it is necessary to maintain our tradition of a society of strong and powerful men and women. Our family has been lucky to not have had to sacrifice a child because of weakness at birth.

Sparticus: Like the other boys of Sparta, I grew up playing rough team games that involved running, jumping, boxing, and wrestling. I will live in the military barracks with the other boys for nine more years, until I am 18. We learn how to endure terrible hardship to become strong soldiers. We sleep on hard beds, wear little clothing, and consume small amounts of food. Although we learn to read and write, our main education is physical and mental endurance. All Spartan boys are taught to tolerate pain, to speak only when spoken to, to then answer in few words, to respect our elders without question, to obey all orders completely, and to strengthen our bodies. It is not uncommon for our trainers to whip us periodically just to make sure we are not becoming weak. I am very proud that my brother and I have proven ourselves worthy. We will both be fine and fearless soldiers.

Zeke: When we become teenagers, our trainers leave us out in the woods without food or shelter, so we can prove that we are capable of surviving on our own. Now I am allowed to grow my hair long as a sign of manliness. I will serve in the army until I am 60.

Amphra: It is not only the men in Sparta who are brave and strong. Only a strong and healthy mother will bear strong and healthy babies. As a girl growing up in Sparta, I too have been trained to be athletic and powerful. Household chores such as sewing and cooking are left up to the slaves. Instead, Spartan girls are raised at home and trained in running, wrestling, and throwing the discus. We also learn to play music, sing, and dance. Many times during the year we have festivals with athletic contests for both men and women. Although they are not as extravagant as those in Olympia, we all enjoy the competition. When I am between the ages of 15 and 20, I will most likely marry. Since women do not see their husbands often, the government encourages us to have more than one husband. This increases our chances of having more babies fit to join the army. I think this is a wise decision on the part of our senate and one reason why we are the most powerful polis in all of Greece.

Sparta and the Persian War *(cont.)*

Diedre: Yes, women in Sparta enjoy many freedoms that are denied elsewhere. We are considered full citizens who can run a business or own land. We enjoy a full public life raising our children and sending them off to war. Although we cannot join the Assembly or become soldiers, we are considered equals and are highly respected throughout the community as having an important role in the future of our city-state.

Narrator 4: Unlike Sparta, Athens did not conquer and enslave neighboring lands to feed its people. Instead it developed other Greek colonies along the shores of the Aegean in Asia. Around 490 B.C., these colonies were invaded by the growing Persian Empire. Athens sent troops to help with the fighting during the Persian wars, but to no avail. The Persian army won and also sent ships back to Athens to punish them for interfering. Athens beat back the Persians in the famous battle of Marathon. Persia vowed revenge and ten years later sailed back to wage battle with Athens again.

Narrator 5: This time the different city-states banded together under the tough leadership of the Spartan army. After years of fighting and huge losses of life on both sides, united Greece was able to defeat Persia. This showed the Greeks what they could accomplish when Athens and Sparta worked together. After the Persian Wars, Athens enjoyed the years of prosperity known as The Golden Age of Athens, which ended when civil war erupted between the two powerful city-states of Athens and Sparta.

Theo: My family lives in a superior polis whose laws isolate us from any outside influence. We are immune to internal corruption because we have few needs, and we are protected by our huge and powerful army. The beauty of our city-state lies in our devoted patriotism and our athletic and military feats. We do not care about cultural contributions or that some consider our lifestyle cruel and harsh. We know that we are highly admired throughout the Greek world for our ability to run an efficient government and for our unbeatable military.

Sparta Activities

After reading information about Sparta and the Persian Wars, complete one or more of the following activities with your class.

Compare the Social Structures

Make an overhead transparency of the chart on page 101. Reproduce a chart for each student to record information about the social structure, government, and economy of Sparta. Discuss and fill out the chart as a class, or divide the class into small groups. Use this same chart later to record information about Athens and to compare the two most famous city-states in Greece.

Dictionary Hunt

Have a student or group of students look up the words "sparse" and "spartan" in a dictionary. Have them present to the class how these words relate to the historical Greek city-state.

Dear Diary

Divide the class into six groups of Spartans: men over 30, men 18–30, boys 7–18, girls, women, and helots. Allow time for each group to discuss what their daily routine might be like in Sparta. Then have each student write a daily diary entry for one week. Make sure students include as much information as possible about what their lives are like in Sparta and their feelings and attitudes toward the polis. Have students share their entries and vote on one example from each group to display in the classroom.

A Spartan Life

Have students draw a Venn diagram to compare their lifestyle at home and at school with the lifestyle of children in Sparta. How are they similar? How are they different? Divide a large piece of paper in half and label one side "Sparta," the other side the name of your community. Have students illustrate some of these similarities and differences.

Strategically Thinking

The battles of the Persian Wars were won because of insightful and strategic thinking. Have students play some strategy games that involve critical thinking skills and planning ahead. These might include "Risk," chess, or checkers. Many math programs also include suggestions for math-oriented strategy games, and the physical education department might also have suggestions for athletic noncontact strategy games.

Society, Family, the Arts, and Education

Compare Social Structures Chart

Name of City-State:_____

Men

occupations

rights and citizenship

family duties

leisure activities

Women

occupations

rights and citizenship

family duties

leisure activities

Boys

education

leisure activities

Girls

education

leisure activities

Government

Economy

Other Interesting Facts

Make a Hoplite Shield

The Greeks were able to oppose the mighty Persian army with the help of *hoplites*, or foot soldiers, who wore helmets and carried long spears, short iron swords, and heavy round shields made from leather, metal, and wood. Have students design and create hoplite shields of their own.

Preparing for the lesson:

1. Divide the class into eight to ten city-state groups. Gather large pieces of cardboard or heavy tagboard so that each group has a piece large enough to make a shield plus enough extra pieces to make a raised border and a center design.

2. Have students make a compass by tying string onto pencils so they can draw large circles to fill the cardboard pieces.

3. Gather large pieces of white construction paper to use as scrap paper for planning their designs. Also assemble heavy-duty scissors, glue, masking tape, and paints. If you wish, students can use metallic spray paint to cover the entire shield and then paint details with acrylic or tempera paints.

4. Bring in pictures of Greek shields. Two good sources include *Ancient Greece* by Powell (Equinox, 1989) and *The Greeks* by Peach (Usborne, 1990).

Teaching the lesson:

1. Tell each group that they are going to design a shield for their city-state's hoplites, or foot soldiers. The shield should use Greek symbols and patterns and somehow represent their city-state in battle.

2. Discuss symmetry and explain that their shield should be symmetrical in four sections around the circular shield's middle symbol. Show examples of Greek shields.

3. Distribute the scratch paper and have students plan the designs for their shields.

4. Distribute the heavy tagboard or cardboard and have students draw their shields with their "compasses." Have them cut out the shields.

5. Have students use the extra shield material to cut out designs and glue them onto their shields. Remind students that the design should repeat itself in all four sections. In the center of the shield should be a symbol representing their city-state.

6. Have students paint their shields and use masking tape to attach the shield to the forearm of a "soldier."

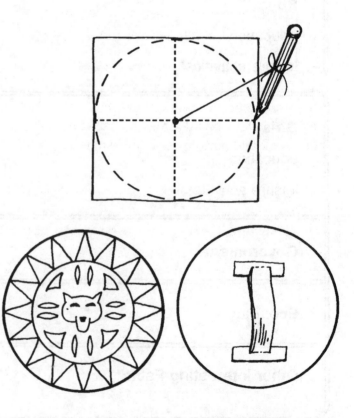

The Golden Age of Athens

Narrators 1–10
Leon, husband and father
Artema, his wife
Zinias and **Trenth**, their sons

Lydia and **Sophia**, their daughters
Hephantus and **Nicias**, their servants
Evanide and **Meno**, business friends

Narrator 1: After the victory of the Persian Wars, Athens enjoyed many glorious years of prosperity under the leadership of a great statesman named Pericles. Pericles had fled from Athens with other citizens during the wars. He later returned and became well-known as a persuasive speaker and intelligent thinker within the Athenian assembly. He was able to convince other Athenians to rebuild Athens and make it stronger than ever. Once he was elected as a high official in the Athenian government, he put three goals into action.

Narrator 2: His first goal was to help protect and defend Athens from future attacks. To accomplish this he had a strong wall built around the city. The wall extended down to the sea. He also increased the size and strength of the navy, making it one of the strongest forces in the Mediterranean Sea region.

Narrator 3: The second goal of Pericles was to rebuild and beautify Athens. He used government money to construct and improve public buildings and temples. Some of these magnificent structures still stand today on the **Acropolis** overlooking Athens.

Narrator 2: Spreading government power more evenly among the social classes and encouraging more active participation by citizens was his third goal. Pericles believed that wealth was something properly used to benefit the community, rather than something for an individual to boast about. He encouraged people with wealth to enable those less fortunate to escape poverty. Pericles established social policies that paid less-affluent Athenians to perform public services. This way, all citizens could afford to take time off from work and participate in decisions important to Athens.

Narrator 3: Under the leadership of Pericles from about 460 to 429 B.C., Athens entered a prosperous time known as the Golden Age of Athens. Let's join a typical middle class farming family as they describe life in Athens during these glory years.

The Golden Age of Athens *(cont.)*

Artema: Good morning! It is not a typical day in our household. Today we are preparing for a **symposium,** or drinking party, tomorrow night. This is an important part of Athenian culture because it is one of the few occasions when small groups of men can meet privately to discuss literature, philosophy, science, history, and mathematics. Since most other events are very public, this gives our family and friends a special time to be together. My husband, Leon, has already left for the coast to trade his olives, and my boys are at school. My daughters, Lydia and Sophia, will help me with the daily chores and preparing for tomorrow's festivities.

Narrator 4: The family lives on a farm just outside the city walls. Although they are not a wealthy family, they live a very content and comfortable life, and the farm supplies most of their needs. The main work revolves around their olive groves, which produce a vast quantity of olives from which they make a variety of olive products. The olives are eaten or mashed for their precious oil, which is used in cooking, cleaning and refreshing the body, and as fuel in clay lamps.

Narrator 5: Olives from the family farm provide for them as food and oil for the family needs and as income when sold in the marketplace in Athens or exported and sold overseas. Although the family has slaves to help with the work, Leon still has much work overseeing sales in Athens and delivery to traders along the coast. This means he spends some time home on the farm, some in town at the market, and some time, like today, visiting the port where the trading boats are docked.

Leon: On trading days I must get an early start, so I can supervise the slaves as they load the large urns of oil onto donkeys. Then we tether the donkeys together and begin our journey. Once inside the city wall, I will meet Evanide and Meno, also traders. We will all travel together through the city streets and down to the coast, while the beautiful **Acropolis** sits high upon the hill above us.

Evanide: The Acropolis was originally a fort. As the city grew and expanded, our ancestors decided to make it the home of the goddess Athena, for whom our polis is named. Her statue stands in the middle of the Acropolis and guards our fine city. Within the Acropolis are many structures and buildings, including the Erectheum and the Great Altar used by the priests for offering sacrifices to Athena during important festivals.

The Golden Age of Athens *(cont.)*

Meno: The largest and most beautiful building within the Acropolis is the **Parthenon,** or temple to Athena. It is 60 feet high and surrounded by 46 graceful columns and more than 500 sculpted figures. It is built entirely of marble and took over 15 years to complete. Inside stands a 40-foot statue of Athena made of gold and ivory. The Parthenon is visible from all parts of the city and has become a landmark of Athens. A pathway called the Sacred Way is the only entrance leading up to the Acropolis.

Leon: About halfway up the Sacred Way stands the theater and temple to Dionysus. Here we have our drama festivals and competitions. Below the Sacred Way is the **Agora,** or marketplace. We will stay far away from this section of the city because it is busy even at this early time in the morning. Finally we will leave the busy city streets through the southwest gate and take the eight-kilometer road that leads to the coast. The high walls on each side offer protection, and we pass many traders coming and going.

Evanide: Once we near the coast we will be able to admire the great *triremes* of the Athenian fleet. These long, sleek ships have great sails and three lines of oarsmen at different levels with armed soldiers riding on top. The long wall to the coast and our strong navy are both a tribute to Pericles.

Meno: Some days we make so many stops to exchange news and discuss current issues that it is well into the afternoon before sales are agreed upon and our wares have been loaded onto the ships docked at the coast. I know Leon is anxious to get back home and help with the plans for his symposium tomorrow night. Evanide and I look forward to the evening and its promise of lively discussions, food, and entertainment.

Leon: My sons wanted to accompany us today, but it was best for them to attend school. When they travel with me on my trading missions, they dawdle and gape at the many people, sights, and boats outside the city. Then we are lucky to return home before nightfall. My wife would have my head if I came home late tonight. If we leave quickly, we can even enjoy a stop at the public bath before heading for our homes.

Narrator 6: The public baths were used by all male metics and citizens of Athens. They were for washing, not swimming, and much better than the large bowls at home that had to be filled by hand from an outside fountain. In the winter the rooms were warmed and the water heated. The men did not use soap. They rubbed olive oil into their skins and scraped off the oil and dirt with a curved tool called a *strigil* before soaking in the water. Many Athenians had a slave in attendance to help cleanse them. The baths served a dual purpose. Much like the gymnasium or Agora, the public baths provided a public meeting place for men to exchange gossip, discuss issues, and enjoy male camaraderie. Leon's boys enjoyed attending the baths so that they could return home and share news with their sisters. But today they are working hard at school.

Zinias: Theo and I began going to school around the age of six. Schools are not public, so we must pay for our education. Father has sent along a slave called a *pedagogue* to watch over us and make sure we work hard. At night our pedagogue makes sure we complete our homework and are prepared for the next day's lessons. Our school is a large room with 20-some-odd boys of all ages gathered in small groups around their teachers. Girls are not permitted to attend school. As you look around the room you can see a variety of activities taking place. One of the groups is practicing some dance steps in preparation for our next festival. My brother and his friend are practicing their music.

The Golden Age of Athens *(cont.)*

Trenth: One of the instruments we learn to play is the **lyre**. Strings are stretched between a straight piece of wood and a surrounding U-shaped wooden frame. The sound is much like a harp. We also learn to play the flute and sing a variety of songs that tell of valiant heroes and the gods. Athenian education requires a mastery of the arts as well as other academic subjects. You can see other groups sitting on wooden stools or benches practicing their reading, writing, and arithmetic.

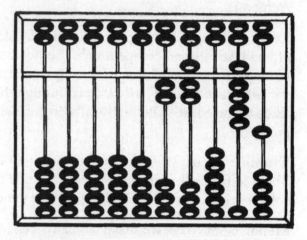

Trenth: We do not use a desk or table to write on. We use a sharpened bronze stick called a *stylus* to scratch into a wax-covered wooden tablet. For important documents we write on paper with reed pens imported from Egypt and ink made from soot and vegetable gum. We learn the Greek alphabet and study many works of literature. The *abacus* is used to help us with our math. It is a wooden frame strung with rows of colored beads.

Zinias: Since I am now 12, after school I will go to the **gymnasium** for physical training. Here I learn how to wrestle, swim, and compete in other athletic and military-style events. An open space in the gymnasium called a *palaestra* is used for wrestling, discus throwing, boxing, and long jumping. Once I reach 15 my physical training will also include skills needed to become a soldier, such as running, leaping, hunting, driving a chariot, and hurling a javelin. At that time my father may place me in a school for higher education. These schools are run by professional *sophists*, who offer instruction in philosophy, astronomy, biology, oration, geometry, and history.

Trenth: By age 18 we complete the last stage of our education by entering the military. Here we learn the duties of citizenship and war. We live together and train together and are constantly supervised. During this stage we are highly respected throughout the community and have a prominent role in festivities. By 21 we gain full citizenship and are released from any parental authority.

Narrator 7: The Athenians valued education. Even though girls, slaves, foreigners, and poor citizens were not included in private school, a well-balanced Athenian education was the best in the ancient world. Girls and women also enjoyed a pursuit of knowledge and the arts, although their training was far less formal and given at home. Lydia and Sophia are home now completing their chores and training.

Lydia: Sophia and I are fortunate to not have to leave home every day for school like our brothers. Our mother instructs us in "domestic science" here at home so that we will be prepared to run households of our own someday. We are taught to read, write, and do simple mathematics. We also learn spinning, weaving, and embroidery. Athenians take great pride in the arts and beauty, so it is important that we become good singers, dancers, and musicians.

106

The Golden Age of Athens *(cont.)*

Sophia: Although we do not participate in physical athletics, we do have many toys and games to entertain us. Our brothers play many ball games, including one that resembles hockey. We have bowling hoops, spinning tops, kites, clay rattles, and jointed dolls. We ride on hobbyhorses and in miniature carts. Our family enjoys playing board games, whose counters or markers are made of clay and bone. Our favorite is a game called *knucklebones*—a game of luck that utilizes the bones of small animals.

Lydia: By the time we are 12 or 13, we stop playing with toys and enter adulthood. A ceremony at the temple dedicates us to the gods. Soon after this many girls get married. Since boys are busy being trained in school and the military, most wives are much younger than their husbands. This is why our training at home is so important. We must be prepared at an early age to look after children, supervise slaves, and skillfully run a household.

Artema: I take great pride in my home and preparing my daughters for marriage. Although Athenian women do not participate in public life, we are highly respected by our husbands and society. Leon often discusses daily affairs with me at the end of a busy day. He takes great pride in the fact that I can reason clearly and that I have my own opinions on many subjects. Wives of citizens cannot own property; we take on the social status of our husband. This is why it is important for Leon to find suitable husbands for our daughters, and to do this, our daughters must be considered a good catch.

Sophia: Soon Father will find me a husband. I know that I have no say in whom he chooses, but I trust and respect his judgment. The man of the house has the ultimate say in such things. He decides whether or not a baby will stay with the family, he disinherits a son who behaves badly, and he controls all business-related family decisions. However, a wife has full charge of household affairs and is admired for running it efficiently.

Artema: We are busy today preparing for a party. Our servants are making sure our home is in top shape and that we will have enough food and good accommodations for our guests. A typical Greek home is made of mud brick one story high. The foundation is stone and the roof is made from baked tiles. Our windows do not have glass, so they are put high up in the walls to keep out dust, heat, and burglars. Our walls are of plaster and hung with colorful tapestries we have woven ourselves. Most of our floors are beaten earth and covered with rush matting and rugs. However, the men's quarters, or *andron*, has a nice mosaic floor.

Lydia: Our rooms are arranged around a central sunny courtyard, the heart of our household. Here we have an altar for offerings and sacrifices to the gods. We also play here, and adults work and gossip here. The number of rooms in a house varies with the family's wealth. Even very wealthy families do not live in high luxury, for we believe that money is best used to improve the state. Country farmhouses such as ours are large and have more land. We have a weaving room where baskets, wool, dye, vats, and looms are kept; a room for cooking on a portable grill, grinding grain and baking in a small clay oven; a room for washing; and a bathroom with a large pot as a toilet that is emptied into a gutter outside.

The Golden Age of Athens *(cont.)*

Sophia: We have separate quarters for the men, women, slaves, and children. We entertain guests in the men's quarters, the most decorated room of the house. It is filled with cushions, couches, and oil lamps.

Narrator 8: The Ancient Greeks had far less furniture and decor than is typical today. Pots and other possessions were hung on the walls instead of placed in cupboards. Personal possessions were kept in baskets and small boxes or chests. Tables and chairs were made from lightweight wood so that they could be portable, and often they were decorated with inlays of ivory, gold, and silver. Couches looked very much like beds and served many purposes. They were for eating, relaxing, and sleeping. Some homes had a family well, but most Athenians sent servants into town to fetch water from the public **fountain house**. Earlier today Hephantus and Nicias, the family's head servants, left for the Agora to fetch supplies for the symposium.

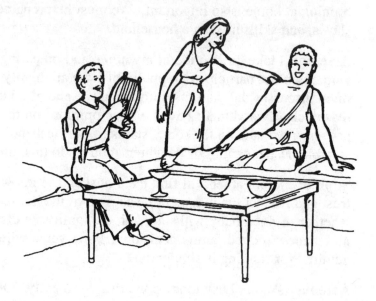

Hephantus: Today we have a long list of errands to perform in town, so we must get an early start. First we prepare the family's light breakfast of bread soaked in wine, figs, olives, and cheese. The Greek diet is fairly simple and healthy. We eat mostly bread, cheese, fruit, vegetables, eggs, and not much meat. Only wealthy people can afford to eat meat often. However, many Greeks live near the sea, so a variety of fish and seafood is popular. Farmers like Master Leon are the heart of our economy. They grow wheat, barley, grapes, and olives. Some farmers keep pigs, sheep, and goats and raise bees for honey.

Nicias: The menu for the symposium is far more extravagant and has many courses. First, we will serve a dish of jellyfish mixed with pine nuts, celery, dates, and oysters. The main course will be tuna flavored with oregano and bay leaves and served with a mixture of peas, beans, turnips, garlic, and onions. The main course will be followed by figs, dates, grapes, cherries, pears, plums, pomegranates, melons, cheese, and cakes sweetened with fruit and honey. Since guests will be arriving soon, the rooms need to be cleaned and swept, and fresh water must be drawn from the courtyard well. The evening meal also needs to be prepared in addition to planning ahead for tomorrow's banquet. While we are at the Agora, the other slaves will set out the familiy's clothing for the symposium.

Hephantus: Athens is a city of contrasts. The old, narrow, dirty streets meander around the Acropolis below beautiful temples that sit high on the hilltop. Athenians do not take much care in adorning their homes, but we place emphasis on expressing ideas and worshipping our gods. We spend a great deal of time in religious activities, festivals, and debating in groups. Government, religion, and ideas come before comfort. Today we are just going to the **Agora**, or marketplace. The Agora also serves as a meeting place for citizens to discuss issues for the assembly. It is a fascinating place filled with foreign traders and businessmen, men or slaves running errands, craftsmen, and citizens debating philosophy and government.

The Golden Age of Athens *(cont.)*

Nicias: Soon we enter the Agora's large open space surrounded by buildings and teeming with people. In the center of the square and covered by canvas awnings are stalls offering all kinds of goods and services. The noise in the Agora is deafening as traders shout to attract customers. Potters, bakers, sculptors, carpenters, smiths, and many other kinds of craftsmen live and work in the city. My favorite shops include the jewelers and cobblers who display their fine wares. I try to avoid the fishmongers; they are the loudest and have the rudest jokes. Lawyers, doctors, and teachers also work in the city, but farther away from the main part of the Agora.

Hephantus: I learn a great deal when shopping with Nicias for he knows a shrewd bargain and can barter well. Soon we are laden with baskets of goods and head for home. First we will stop at the fountain house where it is little quieter and cooler than the streets. Although our family has a well in the courtyard, most townspeople have to carry their water from this communal well. Here we can meet with servants from other homes and catch up with current news.

Narrator 9: Back at the farm Artema and other servants gather the clothes for the party while the girls help prepare dinner. Greek clothing was loosely draped around the body and held together with pins and brooches. Most garments were made from wool or linen, both of which were cool to wear in the hot climate. Men, women, and children all dressed very similarly. The main garment was a tunic called a *chiton*. Some women also wore a *peplos*, or a tunic with a fold at the top. A large cloak called a *himation* was worn outdoors, as were leather sandals or boots.

Artema: Clothes for special occasions like our party tomorrow night are decorated or dyed bright colors such as pink, blue, green, purple, and saffron yellow. I will wear plenty of gold and silver jewelry, including one bracelet inlaid with gems. Athenians place high value on beauty and personal hygiene. We wear long curls or pile our hair high in fashionable waves held by combs and hairbands. Men and women apply scented oils. Leon is now back from trading and the boys will be through with school soon. I will finalize details of the symposium with Leon before the evening meal.

The Golden Age of Athens *(cont.)*

Leon: As our guests arrive dressed in their finest chitons, Nicias will remove their sandals and bathe their feet. Each guest will come with his own body servant to look after his footwear and himations. Although we usually eat together as a family, you and the children will dine elsewhere while I have guests. We men will be served inside the andron. Hephantus has arranged for acrobats and dancing girls to perform for us as we eat and drink our wine. You have truly done a fine job Artema, and make me proud to have such a clever and obedient wife!

Narrator 10: A Greek party host usually employed musicians and dancing girls to amuse his guests. The girls were usually slaves or unmarried women, called hetairai, who were considered good enough to provide entertainment but not to marry. Wine flowed freely at these parties and a game called kottabos was often played. This involved throwing dregs of wine at a saucer balanced on a stand. The men all reclined on their couches and engaged in lively discussions of religion and politics throughout the night. Wives joined their husbands for only two types of events—the theater or a religious festival. Still, for all Athenians, the influence of Pericles made their lives very happy during the Golden Age of Athens.

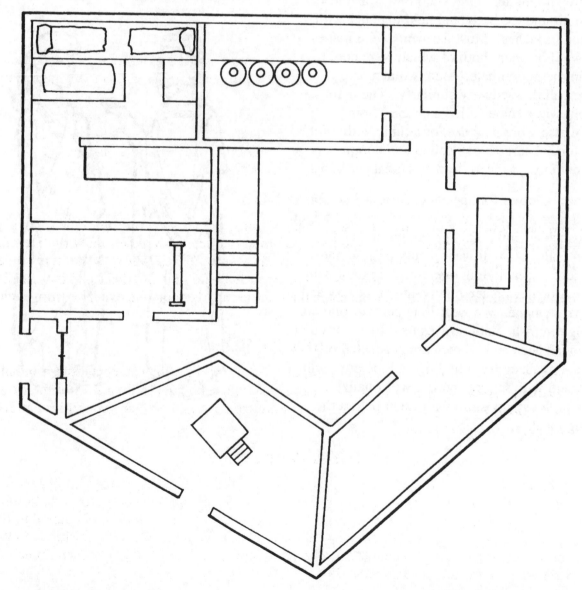

The Golden Age of Athens— Vocabulary and Activities

The following words from the story can be used by students in their Vocabulary Journals (page 5). Remind students to write a complete definition of each word and illustrate them if they wish.

symposium	**gymnasium**	**stylus**
Acropolis	**fountain house**	**Agora**
Parthenon	**public bath**	**lyre**

After reading *The Golden Age of Athens*, complete one or more of the following activities with your class.

Compare the Social Structures

Make an overhead transparency of the chart on page 101. Reproduce a chart for each student to record information about the social structure, government, and economy of Athens. Discuss and fill out the chart as a class or divide the class into small groups. Use it to compare it to Sparta, another famous city-state in Greece.

Greek Word Hunt

Many Greek words were mentioned in the text. Some words, such as *gymnasium*, are still used today. Have students research Greek words to discover how they are used in the English language. and share their findings with the class.

symposium	lyre	sophist	peplos
triremes	abacus	andron	himation
strigil	gymnasium	mosaic	hetairai
pedagogue	palaestra	chiton	

Dear Diary

Divide the class into six groups of Athenians: male citizens, women, servants and slaves, boys, girls, and foreign craftsmen/traders. Allow time for each group to discuss what their daily routine might be like in Athens. Then have each student write a daily diary entry for one week. Make sure students include as much information as possible about what their lives are like in Athens and their feelings and attitudes toward the polis. Have students share their entries and vote on one example from each group to display in the classroom.

Compare the Homes

Distribute a large sheet of white construction paper to each student. Have students fold it in half, then draw and label a typical floor plan of an Athenian home on one half and a floor plan of their own homes on the other half. On the back of the paper have them list at least five similarities and five differences between the homes.

If You Were Pericles

Have a group of students research and report back to the class on Pericles. After learning about his life and achievements, have students write a brief composition describing three ways they could improve their own city. You may want to have students interview members of the local city council to find out specific problems facing their town. Students could also send copies of their compositions to the city council or attend a city council meeting in order to participate in their local government, much like Pericles encouraged his fellow citizens to do.

Greek Architecture

The Ancient Greeks believed that their gods had needs similar to those of mortals. One of these was a place to call home when not on Mount Olympus. Therefore, the Greeks built elaborate temples as homes for their gods. The basic design for the temples was based on the royal halls of the palaces built during the Mycenaean Period. As time went on, temples became larger and more decorative. Many temples or parts of temples have survived the ages and tell us a great deal about Greek architecture.

Early temples had a simple design with square or rectangular floors, ceilings, and doorways. In the front of the temple was a row of **columns** or pillars that formed a front porch. In time, pillars were also added to the back of the temple. Eventually, many temples had pillars around all four sides. These columns or pillars hold up the top structure of the building all the way around the four sides which consists of three main decorated and sculpted areas. The first area is a band called the **architrave**, which was usually painted with a design.

The **frieze** is the band above the architrave and was decorated with relief sculpture. Usually a master sculptor would design the frieze while skilled craftsmen would carry out the work under the master's supervision. Two of the most famous Greek friezes are in the temple of Zeus at Olympia and the Temple to Athena, the Parthenon. The one at Olympia depicts the 12 labors of Hercules. It was common for temples to show figures of gods or heroes in religious or mythical poses. One notable exception is the Parthenon, where the sculptor chose to depict everyday people in Athens. This frieze depicts a festival procession of people accompanying a robe to clothe the statue of Athena. Some people are on horseback and others are walking. Some are even kneeling to tie up their sandals. This frieze gives us today a "snapshot" of what life was like in Athens hundreds of years ago.

Above the frieze is the triangular roof called the **pediment**. This section of the temple was often highly decorated with relief sculpture as well.

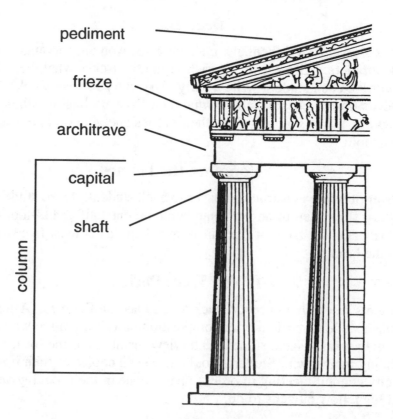

Greek Architecture *(cont.)*

The three main types of Greek architecture are based on the style of the pillars or columns. They are Doric, Ionic, and Corinthian. The top of the column, or the **capital**, can be sculpted in one of these three ways. The **Doric** style is simple and uncomplicated with straight lines. The **Ionic** style shows a pattern with two large ram horns protruding on the sides. The **Corinthian** style is more ornate with complicated carvings showing leaves and flowers. A Corinthian column is much like the columns found in Egyptian temples made to look like lotus blossoms and papyrus. The **shaft**, or main part of a column, has shallow vertical grooves called fluting. In some instances a mixture of styles was used.

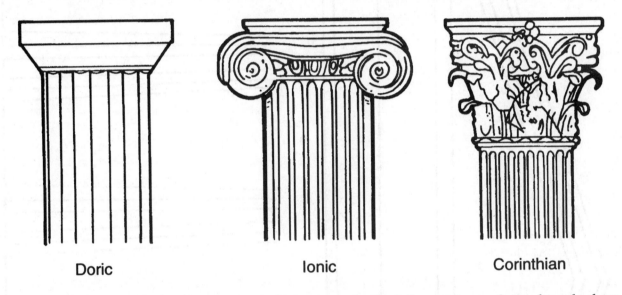

| Doric | Ionic | Corinthian |

Unlike their simple mud-brick homes, the Greeks liked to build their temples to the gods and other religious or governmental buildings in marble and limestone. Fortunately, there was a plentiful supply of marble available in Greece and on the local islands. What is not commonly known is the fact that the Greeks liked to paint their temples in bright colors. Red and blue were the most dominant colors, and gold and green were also often used. These colors have not survived over time, so we generally think of the Greek temples as we see them today—of marble or stone. We can only imagine these fantastic works of architecture perched high upon the Acropolis gleaming down at Athens in their original colored splendor.

Architecture Activities

1. Explore your city to find examples of Greek architecture in homes and government buildings. Why do you think many libraries, courthouses, and other government buildings are designed using these Greek designs?

2. Create a Greek temple of your own. Use the pattern on page 114 to design a temple like one dedicated to a particular god. Draw pictures in the pediment and frieze to reflect aspects of your Greek god. Draw designs in the architrave, and make the capitals of your columns reflect Doric, Ionic, or Corinthian style architecture. Add a doorway and sculptures between the columns. Outline your pictures and designs in thin black marker and then use colored pencils to "paint" your sculpted reliefs, shade with the colored pencils so that your temple looks three dimensional. When you are finished, cut out your temple and mount it on black construction paper. Remember to label it with the name of the god and the type of architecture used.

Create a Greek Temple

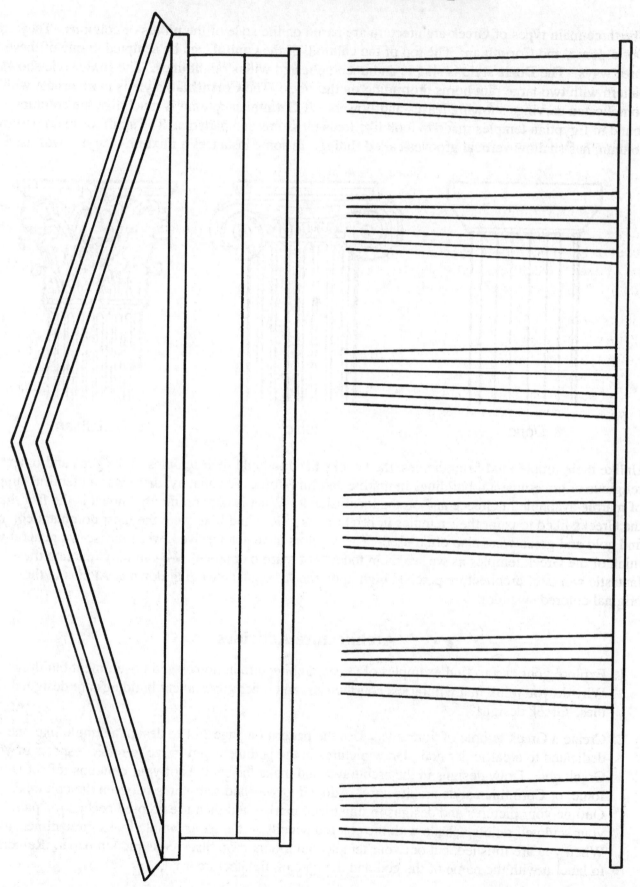

Famous Greek Sculpture

Skilled sculptors were in great demand in Ancient Greece. They were needed to make figures and reliefs for the many temples and government buildings. Statues were also commonly ordered to use to celebrate a victory, pay tribute to a public figure, or depict one of the gods. Unfortunately, only a few examples of Ancient Greek sculpture have survived the centuries. This is partly because sculptors often used stone or marble. Stone becomes brittle over time and eventually erodes away. Marble withstands the elements better, but as with stone, bits and pieces have been chipped away by people. Surviving marble statues or carved reliefs can be found in some museums.

Bronze was another popular material used by sculptors. Bronze statues were made using the "lost wax" or "casting" method. First a basic clay model was made and wooden pegs were stuck into it. Then the clay model was covered with wax so that more intricate details could be carved showing facial features, body structure, and clothing. The model was then again covered in clay with a hole left in the top and bottom. The model was dried and then baked, which hardened the clay and allowed the wax to melt and drip out the bottom. Molten bronze was then poured into the clay cast and left to cool and harden. Finally, the clay cast was broken off to expose the bronze statue.

One advantage to bronze was the fact that different parts of a sculpture or statue could be formed separately and joined to the statue later using weights for balancing. This allowed sculptors to create poses impossible to make using stone or marble. However, a great disadvantage to bronze was its value. The metal was always in demand and easily melted down. Therefore, statues would often disappear to be reused in another project. The stealing and looting of all types of sculpture by enemies posed a continual threat and has contributed to the lack of Greek sculpture today.

Famous Greek Sculpture *(cont.)*

From the surviving pieces, historians can tell that the Greeks were masters at their craft. The most famous sculptor was Phidias. He carved the famous statue of Zeus at Olympia and he probably designed the sculptures located around the Parthenon. Phidias is also responsible for the magnificent gold and ivory statue of Athena displayed inside the Parthenon. In 1972 two bronze statues, each more than six feet tall, were found off the southern coast of Italy by a snorkeler. Since no trace of a shipwreck was found, archaeologists assume the statues were taken as loot from Greece to Rome. The ship must have run into foul weather and the heavy statues thrown overboard to help save the ship. Historians believe these fine specimens are also examples of Phideas great talent.

In order to distinguish Greek sculpture from other types it helps to understand why the Greeks used the art form. Many statues were made as offerings to gods or goddesses, so sculptures usually depicted a god, symbols of a god, or people doing things in tribute to a god. Many statues of nudes depicting Olympic athletes were done in tribute to Zeus and of young girls or ladies in tribute to Athena. The Greeks also carved images of daily life showing popular dress, hairstyles, and activities; heroes in battle and on horseback; and popular public figures. And just as the Greeks loved to paint their temples in vibrant colors, they likewise painted their sculptures.

Make a Plaster Relief Sculpture

Relief sculptures, used to adorn public buildings, were cut as a projected image on a slab. You can make a Greek-style relief carving of your own using white tile grout, a deep Styrofoam meat tray, and simple carving tools such as a large nail, large paper clip, or points of scissors.

1. Mix a batch of white tile grout with water so that you have enough to fill a deep Styrofoam meat tray at least 1 inch (3 cm) thick. (Tile grout is less expensive and less brittle than plaster of Paris.) Let the grout dry completely overnight.

2. Remove the slab of tile grout from the tray and draw a line around the outside edge indicating the depth of the carving. Then use a sculpture tool to etch in the design you will carve on the surface.

3. Carve away the background to the depth-line so that the design stands out from the background. Carefully etch in details onto the design using a sculpting tool, such as a mechanical pencil without lead.

 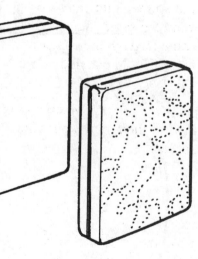 

Make a Clay Oil Lamp

The oil lamp was the only Greek source of light at night. It was made in the shape of a saucer with a spout and handle. Olive oil was burned in the lamp using a piece of cloth afloat in the oil as a wick. Have students create lamps of their own, but make sure you know your fire regulations before lighting up in class. The lamps need not be fired in a kiln to work.

Preparing for the lesson:

1. Be sure you make a lamp and light it before you try this with your class. You may want to give written instructions and have students light them at home with parental supervision.

2. Each student will need a hunk of clay about the size of a softball and clay carving tools, such as a plastic knife, paper clips, mechanical pencils, etc. To light the lamps you will need olive oil, a strip of cloth or braided string for a wick (candle and craft stores actually sell "wick"), and matches.

3. Cover all work surfaces and create an overhead transparency of the lamps at the bottom of the page.

Teaching the lesson:

1. Display on an overhead the examples of lamps found at the bottom of this page. Note that the lamp is shaped like a small bowl or saucer with a handle on one side and a spout at the other. The "bowl" that holds the oil is covered by a decorated lid.

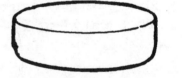

2. Distribute clay to students. Have them set aside ⅓ of their clay to use for the lid. Shape the other ⅔ into a simple low-sided pinch pot.

3. At one end of the pot, pinch the sides together to form a spout. Use a pencil or finger to make sure the spout opens into the "bowl" of the pot. At the other end, pinch the sides together to form a handle.

4. Turn in the top edge of the pot so that a lid can sit on it. Using the remaining clay, form a lid about the same shape and size as the opening to the pot. Make a hole through the center of the lid. Decorate the lid and lamp by carving in patterns or pictures into the clay.

5. Let the lamps dry. Then soak the wick in olive oil and feed it through the spout into the bowl of the lamp. Pour about ½ inch (1 cm) of oil into the bowl so that it feeds the wick. Make sure the wick is not laying in a pool of oil when lit. Place the lid on the lamp and light the end of the wick that sticks out the spout.

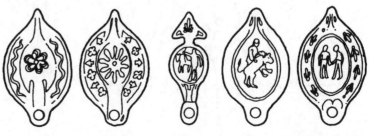

Make a Chiton or Peplos

All Athenians wore the same basic tunic-style dress. Males usually wore an ankle-length *chiton*, although boys, soldiers, and laborers wore knee-length chitons for easier movement. Women and girls wore ankle-length chitons, or a *peplos*. All of these can easily be made using a white or brightly colored sheet or fabric. For added effect, students can decorate the bottom edge with a Greek pattern made with permanent markers or fabric paints.

Make a Chiton for a Male

1. Measure a bedsheet or piece of fabric from the forehead to the knees or ankles, depending on the desired effect. The fabric should be wide enough to fold in two around the body when held from above the elbow to above the elbow.

2. Sew down one side of the fabric to form a large tube. Turn the fabric right-side out, and slip it over the head. Bring the top edge to just below the armpits.

3. Pull the front and back of the fabric together over the shoulders and secure with a large safety pin. Tie a belt, sash, or rope around the waist and blouse the fabric to make it comfortable.

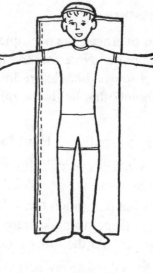

118

Make a Chiton or Peplos *(cont.)*

Make a Chiton for a Female

1. Measure a sheet or piece of fabric that reaches in length from the forehead to the ankles. The fabric should be wide enough to fold in two around the body when held from above the elbow to above the elbow.

2. Sew down the open sides of the fabric, starting 8 inches (20 cm) from the top. On the folded side, cut an 8-inch (20 cm) slit at the top. (This is needed to put the arms through.) Turn the fabric right-side out and slip it over the head so that the top edge runs along the tops of the arms.

3. Secure the fabric in place with several safety pins. Tie a belt, sash, or rope around the waist and blouse the fabric to make it comfortable.

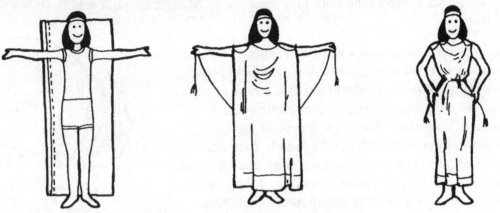

Make a Peplos for a Female

1. Measure a bedsheet or piece of fabric from 12 inches (30 cm) above the head to the ankles. The fabric should be wide enough to fold in two around the body when held from above the elbow to above the elbow.

2. Sew down the open side of the fabric, starting 12 inches (20 cm) opening from the top. Cut a 12-inch (20 cm) slit at the top of the folded side. This will make the folded overflap of the peplos. Turn the fabric right-side out and slip the tube over the head.

3. Fold down the flap on the front and back. Then bring the top edge to just under the armpits. Gather the front and back fabric at each shoulder and secure with large safety pins. Tie a belt, sash, or rope around the waist and blouse the fabric to make it comfortable.

Philosophically Speaking

Hello. My name is Plato and I am here to tell you the story of a great man, who today was sentenced to death. This man was my teacher, Socrates. He was born in Greece in 469 B.C. He had trained to become a sculptor and had studied the sciences of geometry and astronomy. He also pursued philosophy, the love of wisdom. As he educated himself he always worked to understand why things happened in the world. At one time he served in the army as a hoplite soldier, but it was none of these feats that have made him so well-known in our community. He has become famous for being a great teacher and seeker of truth. And it is for these great talents that he was punished.

Had you met Socrates on the street, you would not have imagined that he possessed such a great mind. He was quite unattractive—short and bald with beady eyes and a snub nose. He dressed in rags, and except for his love of fine foods, he shuns most material things and pleasures. He was married late in life to an ill-tempered woman who bore him three sons. Many believe it was from his wife that he learned patience.

All that was important to Socrates was his teaching. He tried to get others to reason by questioning their beliefs and seeking truth. Here in Athens, where we live, a new system of democracy is emerging that affects our whole society. A group of teachers known as "Sophists" has been growing. Sophists do not believe that truth can be found. Instead, they believe that truth is relative, and they deny the existence of universal standards to guide human actions. Many have become paid teachers and instruct young men in subjects such as public speaking, rhetoric, and philosophy. All of these are important skills if one is to have a career in politics. Unfortunately, many Sophists believe that it is more important to argue effectively and persuade others to your side than it is to be right.

Socrates was the foremost critic of the Sophists, for he believed that seeking truth was far greater than anything else. An unpaid teacher, he taught on the city streets so that anyone could approach him and enter into conversation. This is how I first met him. He gathered a following of people who became interested in his teachings. Socrates taught by asking questions in what became known as "Socratic Dialogue" or the "Socratic Method." Socrates would methodically and repeatedly examine someone else's ideas trying to discover truth. He would start by asking a pupil a question and then press mercilessly about why he believed a certain way. More and more questions would be posed and challenged, and answers ridiculed. These dialogues went on for hours and sometimes even days! Many times a student became offended and irate, especially when Socrates pointed out flaws and inconsistencies in his reasoning. To some it may seem that Socrates had a negative purpose, but his real intent was to help others reveal ignorance, observe, analyze, and possibly gain a deeper understanding to rethink beliefs. He was always open minded and was an inspiring teacher.

Philosophically Speaking *(cont.)*

Because of Socrates's continual questioning, some people began to resent him. His methods made them question and reflect upon their own ideas and values, which made them uncomfortable. It also made them aware of their own shortcomings, and they did not like being shown just how ignorant they really were. Some Athenians engaged in power struggles brought serious charges against him. They claimed that he was not religious and that he was corrupting the youth of the polis. They brought him to trial, and still Socrates refused to admit any wrongdoings. He continued to be irreverent, which only irritated his accusers further. A conviction was handed down and Socrates was fined what would be about $1,000 today. He refused to pay and escaped from jail. Then he was offered the choice of being banished from Athens forever or committing suicide by drinking hemlock poison. Although I and many of his other followers pleaded with him to live, he was not afraid of dying and chose the hemlock. He believed that being banished from his beloved Athens was worse than death. I have just watched my dear friend and teacher kill himself. Before his last breath he asked us, his pupils, to continue his teachings.

Although he was an educated man, Socrates never wrote a word during his lifetime and career. So I have now taken a vow to write down all of his teachings and dialogues so that future generations can learn from his wisdom.

Prologue

Plato fulfilled his vow in two famous works, *Socratic Dialogues* and *The Republic*. After Socrates died, Plato traveled throughout the Greek world spreading his teachings. Eventually he began a school called The Academy, where he taught math, science, and philosophy. One of his most promising students was a youth named Aristotle. Aristotle was only five years old when Socrates died. He remained a student with Plato for over 20 years. Eventually he became the tutor of the prominent leader Alexander the Great. Once Alexander was grown and had gone off to fight, Aristotle started his own school, which was funded by Alexander. He collected a variety of plants, animals, poetry, and plays. Aristotle believed that by collecting and studying things he could arrive at the laws of nature, politics, and art. Aristotle is attributed with inventing logic and originating the sciences of zoology, biology, and botany. Socrates, Plato, and Aristotle are considered the three most important figures in Greek philosophy. Their teaching methods and works are still studied today.

Something to Think About

The more we learn about the past, the more we learn about ourselves. Research the following points and formulate an opinion about the questions. Then discuss, write about, or debate with others in a true Socratic dialogue.

1. The problems that Socrates faced with the Sophists are similar to criticisms of our own legal system. Is our judicial system used to discover a person who committed a crime and then punish him or her appropriately, or does it provide an arena for allowing the most persuasive lawyers a method to find ways around the law and perhaps let the guilty go free?

2. The life of Socrates is similar to other great men who had strong beliefs. These men challenged what was currently the standard and many times were punished by authority. Research the following people: Jesus, Mohammed, Confucius, and Buddha. How were their lives similar to Socrates? How were they different?

Socrates' Hot Seat

Socrates was one of Greece's most famous scholars and philosophers. He asked probing questions of his students to try to help them observe, analyze, and think. By doing this he felt the absolute truth could be found. Choose three of the following quotes by well-known philosophers, and explain them in your own words on another sheet of paper. Write a thorough description and be ready to support your reasoning.

1. *Much learning does not teach understanding.* (Herodotus)
2. *Words have a longer life than deeds.* (Pindar)
3. *Time eases all things.* (Sophocles)
4. *A bad beginning makes a bad ending.* (Euripedes)
5. *Know thyself.* (Socrates)
6. *Strive not to become a god; mortal aims befit mortal men.* (Pindar)
7. *The life which is unexamined is not worth living.* (Plato)
8. *Education is the best provision for old age.* (Aristotle)
9. *Nothing in excess.* (Socrates)
10. *All is flux, nothing stays still.* (Herodotus)

Pretend you are at the Agora and that your teacher is Socrates. Take turns taking the "hot seat" in front of the class, just like a pupil of Socrates would be singled out and questioned in front of the gathering. Present one of your quotes and explanations to the group. Then answer the questions posed by "Socrates." "Socrates" will attempt to find contradictions and flaws in your reasoning, so do not get discouraged. Be prepared to defend your position with logical and well-elaborated details that answer "Why?" and "What do you mean?"

What's Your Philosophy?

After Socrates died many other philosophies evolved that may describe a person's outlook on life. Read the descriptions of the philosophies below. Which one best fits your attitude towards life? Why? Write a paragraph on another sheet of paper explaining your reasoning.

SKEPTIC—You reject the idea that truth can ever be found, so you doubt everything.

CYNIC—You believe that we are powerless to control the world, therefore you reject all civilization and want to return to a state of nature.

STOIC—You believe in complete self-control and accept everything that life brings to you since you believe that you cannot control fate.

HEDONIST—You believe that one should seek pleasure and avoid anything that is unpleasant, no matter what the consequences are.

EPICUREAN—You believe that pleasure is good, but one must balance it with work and learning to lead a successful life.

The Golden Age Ends— The Peloponnesian Wars

For many years Sparta feared Athens and its growing power. After the Persian Wars, an alliance of city-states was formed by Athens to help protect Greece from further attacks by Persia. This alliance, called the Delian League, was taken over by Athens during its Golden Age in order to build an empire. City-states outside of Athens were forced to remain in the Delian League and money was collected to help rebuild Athens after the wars. So, as Athens expanded further, Sparta became more and more suspicious and created allies of its own.

In addition to this abuse of power, Athens began attacking cities outside of Greece in order to gain more trade routes. Athens grew in population during the Golden Age and Pericles wanted to ensure food for everyone. Therefore, he conquered land all around the shores of the Aegean Sea, hoping to provide more access to grain and supplies. Finally, in 431 B.C., Sparta had had enough. Backed by its many allies, Sparta threatened to declare war unless Athens agreed to free all of the cities under its control. Athens refused, and so began the bloody Peloponnesian Wars, which lasted more than 20 years.

Athens sent its great army to blockade Spartan towns along the peninsula. In return, the fearless Spartan army marched against Athens, burning and looting its villages. Crops were destroyed and slaves escaped. Pericles attempted to save his people by calling all citizens living outside the city walls to come inside for protection. But the mighty walls of Athens could not save it from disease from within. A terrible plague killed a quarter of the population. Weakened by hunger and so crowded together the disease was able to spread rapidly. Then Pericles died, which left Athens without a leader—helpless and hopeless.

Still, the Athenians continued to fight. In 413 B.C. they attacked Sparta's allies on the island of Sicily. Most of the Athenian army was captured, and the once-powerful navy was destroyed. But even this did not stop the brave Athenians. Remarkably, the war still lasted over nine more years even though Athens never fully recovered from this loss. Athenians melted down gold and silver from their temples to help pay for a new fleet of warships.

Persia had heard of the rivalry and hoped that the two powerful city-states would destroy each other. They gave money to Sparta to build a stronger and faster fleet able to overtake Athens. With this help and poor decision making on the part of Athenian leaders, Sparta finally ended the war in victory.

The Peloponnesian Wars *(cont.)*

What happened? Athenian leaders moved their fleet to a harbor in Hellespont, located on the northeastern corner of the Aegean Sea. The Spartans waited for several days before attacking, to fool the Athenian leaders into believing the harbor was safe. They let smaller ships go to shore for supplies. When they were gone, the Spartans boarded and captured the rest of the fleet. Now the Spartans backed by the powerful Persian Empire blockaded the city of Athens, cutting off its food supply by land and sea. The Athenians eventually surrendered in 404 B.C.

Although Sparta's allies demanded that Athens be destroyed and its people made slaves, Sparta decided to leave the city intact. But the end of the rivalry did not bring peace or unity back to Greece. The Spartan kings threw out Athenian democracy and set up a system of tyrants. These tyrants were disliked and eventually overthrown by the Athenians, who attempted to re-create a democracy. This time the democracy did not unite the people. Many young citizens refused to take part in public affairs. Others became highly suspicious of anyone displaying antidemocratic attitudes. It was during this time that the great philosopher Socrates was condemned and put to death for his teachings.

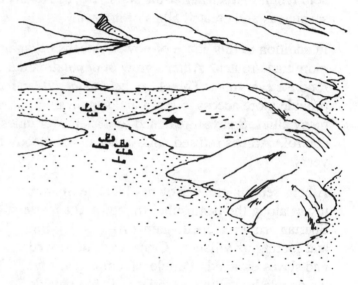

For many years smaller wars between various city-states continued. It finally took a force 50 years later and outside of Greece to bring harmony back to the country. To the north of Greece lay Macedonia, whose kings were slowly invading and conquering the surrounding lands. Under the leadership of King Philip II, Greece was united with Macedonia by 337 B.C. When Philip died, his son Alexander took over and made the Greek Empire the greatest the world had ever known.

What Do You Know?

1. Why did Athens form the Delian League? How did the league change? How did this contribute to the Peloponnesian Wars?

2. What were some factors that weakened Athens? Do you think Pericles made a wise decision to call the people inside the city walls? Why or why not?

3. What factors outside Athens helped Sparta to win the war? Why did Persia help if they were an enemy of Greece?

4. What happened to Greece after the Peloponnesian Wars?

5. How do you think the wars could have been avoided?

Comparison Writing and Debate

Athens and Sparta were two powerful but very different Greek city-states. Eventually their differences led to the Peloponnesian Wars. Have students compare and contrast the lifestyle of the Spartans to that of the Athenians.

Preparing for the writing lesson:

1. Make an overhead transparency of The Writing Process (page 17).

2. Make an overhead transparency of the Compare/Contrast Chart (page 127) to model the prewriting activity for students.

3. Reproduce an Editing Checklist (page 18) and a Compare/Contrast Chart for each student.

4. Write the compare/contrast words (page 126) on the chalkboard or on a chart.

5. Have students take out their Comparing Social Structures (page 101) charts for both Sparta and Athens.

Teaching the writing lesson:

1. Review the two Comparing Social Structures charts as a class. Tell students that they are going to use that information to write a composition describing the similarities and differences between the two city-states.

2. Review the Writing Process and distribute the Compare/Contrast Charts for students to use for the prewriting stage of their composition.

3. Display the overhead transparency of the Compare/Contrast Chart. Have students write "Athens" for Subject #1 and "Sparta" for Subject #2. Then have students choose at least five categories for comparison from their Comparing Social Structures charts and write these categories down the center column.

4. Have students write brief supporting details from their research onto the Compare/Contrast Chart for each category. Tell students to include as many details as possible when actually writing their composition.

5. Discuss with the class the steps for using the Compare/Contrast Chart to help write their compositions. Point out that the introduction should give the reader some interesting background that will make him/her want to read the rest of the composition. The introduction should also let the reader know the names of the two subjects being compared (Athens and Sparta).

6. Tell students to begin a new paragraph to tell about the first category. The paragraph should open with a sentence describing the category. Then it should describe all of the supporting details for one subject (Athens), and then all of the supporting details for the second subject (Sparta).

7. A new paragraph should incorporate each category of comparison. Review with students the compare/contrast words and encourage them to use a wide variety of words in their composition.

Comparison Writing and Debate *(cont.)*

8. Explain to students that their conclusions should restate the names of the two subjects (Athens and Sparta), give a short summary that describes what the composition was about, and provide any closing remarks.

9. Have students follow the Writing Process as they write their compositions. Review the Editing Checklist to remind students of the steps needed to improve their rough drafts before making their final drafts.

10. Once completed, have students share their compositions and choose a few examples to display in the classroom. You may wish to use this format for other assignments appropriate for comparison writing.

Words that Compare: *same, similar, also, alike, in common, each, too, much, like, as well as, similarly, likewise,* and *both.*	**Words that Contrast:** *different, differ, differently, differences, however, yet, on the other hand, although, but,* and *unlike.*

As a follow-up or alternative to the writing lesson, divide the class into two groups and lead a debate as to which polis would have been their choice to live in.

Teaching the debate lesson:

1. Have students review the information they gathered on their Comparing Social Structures charts for both Sparta and Athens.

2. Ask students to decide which city-state they would have rather lived in had they been born in Ancient Greece. Have students write their name and choice on a scrap piece of paper and turn it in. This will permit groups to be made based on their choice and not friends. Divide the class into the two groups.

3. Tell the groups to write down information that describes the benefit of living in their polis. Have them also write down disadvantages of living in the other polis. Make sure each student in the group can support the benefits or disadvantages with logical details.

4. Once the groups have had time to discuss their positions and supporting arguments, bring them together and use the following format to lead a debate.

   A. Flip a coin to decide which group goes first. Assign a timer to stop a speaker at exactly three minutes.

   B. Have the first group choose a speaker to describe one benefit of living in their polis.

   C. Have the other group choose a speaker to debate that specific argument. Then a speaker from the second group chooses a speaker to speak about a benefit of living in their own polis.

   D. The debate continues in this fashion until no further points can be made or argued. Make sure all speakers from the group get a chance/are required to participate.

5. Discuss the outcome of the debate. Lead students to discover and talk about choices or values they might based on today's standards that might be different from those of people in Ancient Greece.

Compare/Contrast Chart

Introduction:		
Subject #1:		**Subject #2:**
Supporting Details	**Categories**	**Supporting Details**
Conclusion:		

Strategy Skills

Have students play a game that will sharpen their strategy skills.

Preparing for the game:

1. Gather 12 markers of any kind (checkers, rocks, blocks, etc.).

2. Set up a game on the chalkboard or overhead projector that will pit you against the entire class so they will understand the rules.

Playing the game:

1. Arrange the 12 markers so that there is a row of three, a row of four, and a row of five markers. Label the first row Macedonia, the second row Thessaly, and the third row Peloponnesus.

2. Tell students that the object of the game is to "capture" all the markers, but to NOT be the one who takes the last marker.

3. During a turn one or more markers may be removed from any one row. This means they could even take the entire row if they choose.

4. They may NOT take markers from more than one row during a turn.

5. Play the sample game. The game might go something like this:

    Teacher takes marker(s); students take marker(s); teacher; students, etc.

    Whoever must take the last marker loses the game.

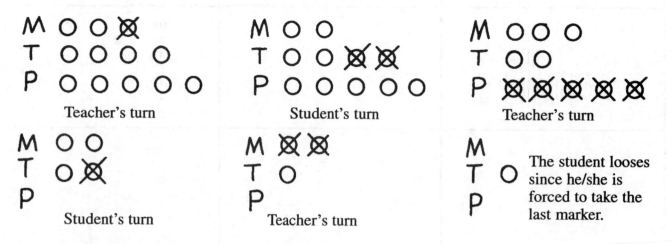

6. Play a few times against the class. Take turns going first or second. Remind students to plan ahead or predict what the next moves should be in order to win.

7. Have students gather items for markers and play against one another. As they play, have them look for patterns that allow a person to win.

Alexander the Great

Under the skillful leadership and personal philosophy of Alexander of Macedonia, Greece was able to acquire an empire unparalleled in the ancient world. Have students participate in a cooperative group activity to learn more about this fascinating leader in Greek history.

Preparing for the lesson:

1. Divide the class into cooperative groups with five students in each group. Make sure each group's members represent a balance of learning styles and reading abilities.

2. Reproduce five copies of Alexander the Great, Parts 1–5 (pages 130–134) so that there is one packet for each group.

3. Reproduce an Inference Chart (page 135) for each student to record their findings.

4. Organize the classroom desks so that there are areas for groups to meet, read, and discuss the information.

Teaching the lesson:

1. Tell the cooperative groups that they are going to read about a great leader in Greek history—a man known as Alexander the Great. However, rather than every student reading all of the information, each student will read a portion of the information and report back to the group. This is called "jigsaw reading."

2. Distribute the packets of information and allow time for the cooperative groups to decide who will be responsible for each section.

3. Distribute the Inference Charts and explain that this page will be used to record information found in each section.

4. Have students regroup. All students who have chosen Part 1 will form a Part 1 discussion group. Do this for each part. Tell them they may take turns reading aloud, read in partners, or just read silently in a group together—however they choose to make sure all students read the same information.

5. When each student in a discussion group has finished reading, the group will talk about the content of the passage and record their findings on the Inference Chart. Check with each discussion group to make sure they are taking turns speaking and that everyone is contributing to the group.

6. After all of the discussion groups have read, discussed, and recorded their information, they will return to their original cooperative groups.

7. Allow time for each member to summarize the content of their part and share what their discussion group recorded on the Inference Chart. Each member in the cooperative group can use this information to record in the appropriate section on his/her own Inference Chart as it is shared. Together as a cooperative group, they will answer the questions at the bottom of the page.

8. Once all groups have finished, review the page as a class and discuss the conclusions the students made about Alexander the Great.

Alexander the Great *(cont.)*

Part #1—King Philip II of Macedonia and The Birth of Alexander

Macedonia was a large state to the north of Greece. For many years Macedonia did not pose a threat to Greece because it was far less organized and lacked strong leadership. However, when King Philip II took the throne in 359 B.C., he changed history forever.

King Philip II turned Macedonia into a mighty military power by establishing a paid professional army of highly trained, full-time soldiers. He also caused advancements in strategy, battle formations, and weaponry, such as towers on wheels that enabled soldiers to attack high walls, battering rams that could be used to smash through locked gates, large catapults able to hurl heavy rocks, and smaller catapults that could throw several flaming spears at once. Philip used his powerful army to conquer lands and build an empire.

In 356 B.C., King Philip II and his wife Olympia, had a son, whom they named Alexander. He grew up a brave and intelligent boy who displayed strong leadership qualities. One famous tale describes such a time when Alexander was only 14 years old. King Philip had brought home a fiery black horse to add to his stable. When Philip tried to mount the steed, it bucked and reared, throwing its head back and forth and kicking its legs. The king was immediately thrown off, and he decided that the horse was useless. He called for it to be taken away.

Alexander had been among the crowd watching from the sidelines. He stepped forward and insisted that the great horse was being wasted. Many onlookers considered Alexander's remarks to be bold and impudent because he was only a youth. But the king challenged Alexander to tame the horse and promised him he could keep it if he was successful.

According to the legend, the horse instantly calmed when Alexander approached. He patted the stallion's neck and spoke softly in his ear. Amazingly, the horse allowed Alexander to lead him. Alexander had noticed that the horse did not like the sight of his great shadow upon the ground. Gently he turned the horse away from its shadow and was able to swing into the saddle without resistance. Alexander rode away and back to his father.

The crowd applauded this victory and his father wept in joy. The king gave his son the horse, Bucephalus, saying, "My boy, you must find a kingdom big enough for your ambitions. Macedonia is too small for you." These were prophetic words.

Bucephalus was proud and loyal, allowing no one but Alexander to ride him as long as he lived. According to legend, the horse would even lower his body to let Alexander mount him more easily. For years Alexander rode the valiant horse and friend into many battles. When the horse became too old for fighting, Alexander still rode him proudly near the battle lines, then switched to a stronger horse for fighting.

This legend describes some of the special qualities that Alexander had that allowed him to conquer lands and still maintain respect as a great leader: observation and determination, willingness to give in to the needs of others in order to gain ultimate control, compassion, and respect.

Alexander the Great *(cont.)*

Part #2—Alexander's Youth and Education

King Philip II of Macedonia wanted the best education possible for his son. The king had always felt an Athenian education was the finest in the ancient world, so he began a search for the wisest man in Greece to be Alexander's tutor. Many intelligent men applied for the position, but none were educated in the high culture of the Athenian city-state.

Then King Philip heard of Aristotle, widely known as the greatest thinker alive and Plato's prize student. Aristotle, now in his early forties, accepted the king's invitation to come to Macedonia and teach his 13-year-old son. With the king's unlimited funds, Aristotle created throughout the kingdom an atmosphere for learning unlike any before.

Aristotle was interested in everything and sought ways to understand the world and humankind's role within it. He investigated the fields of biology, botany, zoology, astronomy, physics, mathematics, psychology, rhetoric, logic, politics, and ethics, as well as the fine arts of literature, music, and drama. He gathered extensive collections of plants, animals, books, and other things that would help him learn. He had an encyclopedic mind.

Alexander was an excellent student with a quick mind. He devoured books on Greek literature and poetry. He showed a great thirst for knowledge in all areas and became determined to spread this knowledge around the empire. While on military campaigns for his father he would observe the plants and animals of the region. He kept detailed records and collected specimens to send home to Aristotle. It is said that he even tagged wild deer in order to study their lifespan. As he got older, Alexander would also take architects, scholars, naturalists, and artists on his missions. As the armies fought, these workers studied, mapped, calculated, constructed, and recorded what they learned in order to help Alexander better understand and maintain his expanding empire.

Alexander was extremely interested in philosophy and justice. He enjoyed long discussions with Aristotle about the best way to live, to govern, and to behave towards one's subjects and friends. His education was furthered by close contact with international diplomats and wise people in his father's court. Alexander determined that it was best to not only respect nature, but also to respect the need of people to be treated as equals regardless of their culture. He used this philosophy to rule fairly as he conquered other lands. His goal was to create a unified world in which there would be harmony between the East and West. He blended Greeks and non-Greeks together in his armies and administration. He was able to establish over 70 cities. There is little doubt that Aristotle greatly influenced Alexander. He set high standards for his star pupil and taught him to "be what you wish to seem."

Alexander the Great *(cont.)*

Part #3—Alexander, Leader in Battle

Alexander showed great character and leadership while growing up in Greece. By age 16 he served as a regent for his father, King Philip II of Macedonia, and subdued an uprising of Illyrian tribes. Together they conquered the lands to the north and west of Macedonia. Then they turned south toward Greece. The Greeks, weakened by their own civil war, were no match for the newly strengthened Macedonian army. In 338 B.C., at the age of 18, Alexander spearheaded his father's victory at Chaeronea, making King Philip II the new ruler of Greece.

Alexander proved to be a brave soldier at Chaeronea and exposed himself to danger in ways no responsible commander should do. But he did it again and again. Many called him fearless; others called him lucky. Many tales about his valor have been told and retold.

During the siege, Alexander worked on a high mound preparing his war machines of catapults and battering rams to overtake the city walls. While atop the mound, a large bird of prey dropped a stone on his head. Most likely the bird mistook Alexander's helmet for a tortoise and dropped the stone in attempt to crack the shell and get at the meat inside. Alexander was fortunate to walk away unharmed, yet his orator advised him to watch his safety for this must surely be a sign of warning and danger.

Alexander showed great restraint during the battle until he saw that his men were being attacked on the wall. Then, without hesitation, he dashed to their side, fighting mercilessly. Suddenly, a man whipped out a dagger and struck him. Although the blow should have killed Alexander, he continued hacking away at oncoming enemies. Perhaps he thought that this was the danger he had been warned to avoid, and, now that it was over, he could proceed to fight without further harm.

He was wrong. An arrow shot from atop the wall sank deep into Alexander's shoulder. He was dragged from the front lines while a doctor pulled it out. His shoulder bled heavily and was wrapped in dressings. The doctor urged Alexander to lay still and rest, but Alexander felt the tug of duty and rejoined his troops.

The dressings slipped off his shoulder while fighting, and blood poured out from beneath his armor until finally he fainted. Alexander was carried off the field delirious and pale. He was forced to remain out of the battle, but he continued to direct his troops from the sidelines until he regained strength and could fight again.

Stories such as these made others respect the youth and vow to follow his leadership. It was not long until he would need such loyalty. Just two years after Greece was conquered, King Philip II was assassinated. At the age of 20, Alexander became King of Macedonia and Greece, with the responsibility of carrying on his father's legacy to expand the empire.

Alexander the Great *(cont.)*

Part #4—Alexander Conquers Persia

Alexander was a young man of 20 when his father, King Philip II of Macedonia, was assassinated in 336 B.C. Already a skilled leader, he quickly put down rebel forces that revolted. Now that he was the ruler of the Macedonian and Greek empires, he combined the troops to face their biggest challenge ever—the great Persian Empire.

In 334 B.C., Alexander crossed the Dardanelles to begin his conquest of Persia. King Darius, an ancestor of the king who had originally attacked Greece during the Persian Wars, was no match for Alexander and his forces. During the next 12 years Alexander's troops marched, fought, conquered, and expanded his empire throughout the Mediterranean region, Asia, and India. Historians today still study Alexander's battle techniques and strategies.

One tale describes Alexander and his troops as they came upon thousands of Greek slaves on the road to Persepolis in Persia. These Greeks had once been citizens of Greek colonies in Asia Minor and had been made slaves by the Persians. During the confusion of war they had escaped the city and were now looking for refuge. Many of these Greeks had been treated harshly during their capture, not uncommon in the ancient world. Some had their hands, feet, ears, or noses cut off. Some had been branded, and many were left with only the limbs needed to perform their craft or labor.

Alexander was struck by the sight of these men and wept openly. He offered to help them get back to Greece, but they refused. Their pride would not let them return in such a degraded physical state. Instead, they pleaded with Alexander to give them some land where they could live together, tilling the soil and working their crafts. Alexander agreed and also provided them with money, seeds, livestock, clothing, and shelter.

Alexander proceeded to Persepolis. After seeing the atrocities committed on their fellow Greeks, many of the soldiers were eager to destroy and loot the city. It was custom in the ancient world for soldiers to be rewarded for their hardships and loyalty to their leader with the spoils of victory. Alexander allowed them but one day to plunder the city, but he refused to allow his troops to kill all the people and destroy the city out of revenge. He issued orders that the people should be spared and that the women should keep the jewels that they wore.

Alexander created a great legacy with his vast empire. It stretched from Greece in the west to India in the east and encompassed Greece, Asia Minor, Persia, and Egypt. He had fought hard and suffered many wounds. In June of 323 B.C., Alexander suddenly became sick and retreated to the city of Babylon. A few days later he was dead. The man who had ruled the ancient world was not yet 33 years old.

Alexander had established over 70 cities from which his people could administer his vast empire. Many of these cities carried the name Alexander, including Alexandria, Egypt, which served as a center of trade and learning for centuries. During his lifetime, Alexander became known as Alexander the Great. For more than a thousand years after his death Alexander's life and conquests continued to be a popular subject for music, art, and literature throughout Egypt, India, and Persia.

Alexander the Great *(cont.)*

Part #5—Alexander's Legacy

Because Alexander had been educated as a Greek by his teacher, Aristotle, his attitude towards conquered people was new and innovative. As he conquered new lands throughout the Mediterranean region, Asia Minor, and Persia, he established colonies modeled after Greek cities. He knew he could not maintain complete control over these colonies with force alone. Therefore, as his armies moved on, Alexander left behind Greeks to build a governing city and rule the land.

In addition, Alexander believed in treating conquered people as equals. In most cases he allowed the native leaders to retain their authority. He allowed the people to keep practicing their local religions. And he encouraged everyone to adopt a philosophy of understanding and tolerance. Alexander himself began wearing Persian clothing and urged his men to worship him as a god, as was customary of Persian kings. He married a daughter of his Persian enemy, King Darius. Alexander encouraged the Greeks in authority to marry native women, adopt native customs, and in general blend into the new world they were creating. Alexander hoped that by doing this the local people would consider Greek rule as kind and fair and that they would be more willing to comply with it.

This philosophy proved highly successful. Most people did not rebel, and Greek culture spread throughout the known world. Alexander created a commonwealth of peoples with Greek as a universal language. All across the new empire people worshipped Greek gods and learned Greek literature. The influence of the Greeks became so widespread that the period from Alexander's rule to 100 B.C., long after his death, became known as the Hellenistic Era, which means "Greek-like."

The Hellenistic Era was a time of magnificent accomplishments. Greek teachings in the areas of science, art, literature, and philosophy became the norm. In many areas, such as Egypt and Persia, people adopted two systems of life instead of blending together. People who lived in the Greek-ruled cities adopted Greek ways, while people who lived in the country outside the cities often kept their native customs and religion.

During this period the center of Greek culture shifted from Athens to the new city of Alexandria, Egypt. Here a 370-foot lighthouse was built in the harbor. This magnificent structure was one of the Seven Wonders of the Ancient World. A huge museum there became the intellectual center of the world—a place where mathematicians, scholars, astronomers, scientists, poets, and philosophers could gather and explore further learning. A great library of more than 500,000 papyrus scrolls in both Greek and non-Greek languages was established. Some scientists believe that the oldest existing manuscript of the Old Testament was first translated here.

Greek culture flourished, but politically Alexander's gigantic Greek empire broke apart after his death. No single leader was powerful enough to take his place. Five generals divided the empire amongst themselves into at least 34 different kingdoms, thus splintering and diluting their power. Neither before nor since has anyone had the power over such a vast kingdom as did Alexander the Great.

Inference Chart

Complete the chart with your findings as you read about Alexander the Great.

Part	How does this affect or reflect his leadership?	How does this affect or reflect his character?
#1—Alexander's Birth		
#2—Youth and Education		
#3—Leader in Battle		
#4—Conquering Persia		
#5—Alexander's Legacy		

Answer the following questions on the back of this page using complete and well-elaborated sentences.

1. How was King Philip II of Macedonia able to create a mighty military force?

2. Why was Alexander so successful at spreading his empire?

3. What strategies allowed Alexander to be accepted by those he conquered?

4. What lasting contributions were made by Alexander the Great?

5. Why did the empire break apart after Alexander's death?

The Who and What of Ancient Greece

Long before Ancient Greece even existed, most people believed that the gods were responsible for all that happened on Earth. Even most of the Ancient Greek people thought so, but there was a growing number of highly educated individuals who continually searched for answers to their questions by observing their world around them. For the most part, these scholars had little influence over society as a whole. However, their influence and contributions to knowledge and ways of thinking were considerable.

Biology, Botany, and Zoology—Aristotle, the great philosopher and teacher of Alexander the Great, is attributed with founding these areas of scientific study. He was known for his vast collections of plants and animals. He believed that people could learn more about Earth, nature, and themselves through observing, recording, and rational thinking. Another Greek scientist, Xenophanes, understood that fossils were the remains of plant and animal life preserved in rock.

Medicine and Physiology—For centuries any illness or disease was thought to be punishment by the gods, so people went to priests for help in curing disease. Patients often made clay terracotta or bronze models of their diseased body parts to offer them to the gods. Models of legs, eyes, ears, breasts, and noses have been found at shrines. In particular they made offerings to the god of medicine, Asclepius, and traveled to his most famous temple at Epidaurus. According to legend, Asclepius was the son of Apollo. He was raised by a centaur who taught him the art of healing. He was usually depicted holding a large stick with a snake curled around it, the symbol of medicine later given to Hermes by Apollo to carry as his wand in flight. At the temple in Epidaurus large numbers of sick people came to be looked after by the priests of Asclepius, who treated them with magic spells while they slept and prescribed special diets, exercises, and baths.

By the 5th century B.C., schools of medicine were established. Their emphasis was on discovering how the physical body functioned and how to cure disease. Hippocrates was one doctor who practiced a more scientific approach to medicine. He would begin each treatment by finding out as much as possible about the patient: their age, type of work, behavior, and sleep patterns. Then he would ask about the symptoms the patient was experiencing. Over the years he developed a system of diagnosing and the methods of treatment a doctor should follow with different illnesses. He also wrote a pledge about the duty of doctors, called the Hippocratic Oath. Medical doctors still take a version of this oath today. Another doctor named Herophilus began dissecting bodies to learn about the nervous system.

Many doctors in Ancient Greece followed the practice of taking blood from a patient. They believed this would take the disease out of the body. They operated on the body with surgical instruments such as forceps, knives, and probes made of bronze and iron. Powerful herbs, such as opium and the root of the mandrake were used as anesthetics. But these were not very effective and made having an operation a very painful and dangerous experience.

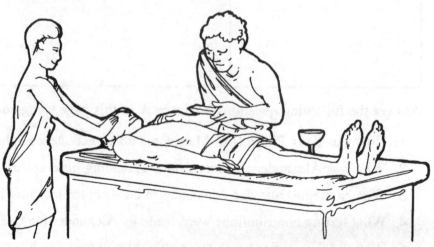

The Who and What of Ancient Greece *(cont.)*

Mathematics—Mathematical calculations were mainly used for measuring distances, surfaces, and curves on and beyond Earth. They were also used in building or construction. Most early Greek mathematics were some form of geometry. Pythagoras was a mathematician who experimented with numbers by using pebbles until he finally worked out his famous theorem on the relative lengths of the sides of a right triangle. He also discovered that the notes of a musical scale in music are mathematically related to the length of the string plucked or the pipe blown into.

Physics and Engineering—The Greeks' skill in engineering and physics is best demonstrated by their beautiful temples. The columns that formed the tall colonnades around buildings were massive stone cylinders held together by metal pegs. The heavy stones were lifted into place using a system of ropes and pulleys. Other simple machines, such as inclined planes and levers, were also used. The screw was used by the inventor Archimedes as a device to raise water from one level to another. A handle was turned, trapping water along grooves and moving it up along the edge of the screw. Pumps like this are still used in Africa today. Archimedes is also attributed with the discovery of the displacement theory. He noticed the water level rise and fall when he got in and out of his bath. He realized that his body displaced its own volume of water. He went on to further experiment with the theory to form new ways to measure volume using displacement.

Astronomy and Geography—Many advances in astronomy were made by the Greeks. Most of them were disbelieved and condemned by society and then proven true by future scientists. The astronomer Aristarchus discovered that the Earth moved around the sun, a theory that was scorned for thousands of years. Anaxagoras believed that the moon did not shine itself, but rather reflected light from the sun. Hipparchus located and charted over 850 stars and noted changes caused by Earth rotating on its axis. Hipparchus also contributed to a more scientific approach to map-making and geography. Now a map-maker could locate a point on the earth by relating it to the positions of stars and other celestial bodies. Calculations were made based on astronomy and land features using the meridian and lines of latitude. Eratosthenes calculated the circumference of the Earth by measuring the angle of the sun at Alexandria in northern Egypt and measuring the distance from there to Syene in the south when the sun was overhead at noon. His figure for the circumference was off by only 320 km. The study of the surface of the Earth became known as geography.

Who Did What?

The object of this game is to correctly identify 12 Greek contributors to science, art, and mathematics. Use the following rules while playing:

1. Decide as a class whether you will play as individuals, partners, or teams.

2. You may use any information from this unit, your social studies book, a dictionary, or encyclopedia to help you find answers.

3. You may only turn in your answers once. Make sure you have checked all information carefully and did not just guess based on the first letter of the name given.

4. The first one to record and turn in 12 correct answers is the winner.

Sappho	Thales	Sophocles	Ptolemy
Hipparchus	Archimedes	Eratosthenes	Hippocrates
Strabon	Empedocles	Euclid	Pythagoras

Read the information in the following boxes that describe some famous Greeks. Research the identities and write the person's name on the line. The first letter of each name has been provided for you.

---

1. A _____

He lived about 287–212 B.C. He was an astronomer, inventor, and mathematician. He studied at the museum in Alexandria and spent the latter part of his life in Syracuse. He discovered an important law of physics called the Theory of Displacement, which proves that an object displaces its own volume of water. He invented a type of pulley and a screwlike device for raising water.

---

2. E _____

He was the first known physicist. He attempted to explain the principles of motion. He described how all things come from a combination of four elements: earth, fire, air, and water—a much different view from that held by earlier thinkers.

---

3. E _____

He lived from about 275–195 B.C. He made many contributions to the study of geography. He attempted to calculate the circumference of the earth using the angle of the sun. His calculations proved to be reasonably accurate.

Who Did What? *(cont.)*

4. E _____

He moved to Alexandria to establish a mathematics school. He created a system for the study of geometry and wrote 13 books called the "elements." He is known as "the father of geometry."

5. H _____

He was born about 190 B.C. in Nicea and is known as the greatest astronomer of ancient times. He built an observatory in Rhodes and cataloged over 850 stars. He compiled and examined all of the records of astronomers before him. He noted changes on Earth such as how it rotates on its axis and how this affects the seasons. He was the first person to record the positions of the stars by lines of latitude and longitude. He also made more accurate measurements of the distances of the sun and moon from the Earth than anyone before him.

6. H _____

He lived from about 460–377 B.C. He was a doctor and wrote about medicine. He founded a famous mathematics school 50 years after the death of Pythagoras that lasted over 200 years. He wrote the first known book on geometry, which made it easier for students to study the subject. He founded the most famous medical school on the island of Cos. He separated medicine from philosophy, religion, and magic. He believed in making observations, recording data, and basing remedies on what was known about the body. His oath regarding the responsibility of a doctor is still taken today by physicians.

7. P _____

He lived from about A.D. 100–170 and became one of the most famous astronomers ever. He wrote a book called "Geography," which applies his knowledge of astronomy to geography. He located cities and other places of interest by using latitude and longitude. He was one of the first to represent the curved surface of the Earth on a flat plane and show a primitive outline of the Earth. He gathered important data from previous astronomers and published it in a 13-volume book called "A Mathematical Composition."

8. P _____

He lived from about 560–500 B.C. and is the most famous Greek linked to geometry. He established a mathematics school and developed the theorem for calculating the sides of a right triangle.

Who Did What? *(cont.)*

9. S _____

She was born around 612 B.C. on the island of Lesbos and later moved to Sicily. She became one of the greatest Greek poets and founded a school for girls. She wrote nine books of poetry and finally died in the middle of the 6th century B.C.

10. S _____

He lived from 496–405 B.C. and was an Athenian writer of 123 tragic plays. He won many prizes at the Festivals to Dionysus in Athens. He was one of the first to write plays that contained more than two characters and used stage scenery. He wrote "Antigone," "Oedipus," "Tyrannus," and "Electra."

11. S _____

He was born around 64 B.C. and wrote "Geography," in which he tried to include everything known about geography up to that time. He was one of the first anthropologists. He had a special interest in the way that people lived and would examine a particular region to describe their lifestyle—their values and beliefs, what they ate, their clothes, and their homes. He recorded a great deal of information concerning the location of mountains, rivers, valleys, and cities as well as earthquakes and volcanoes.

12. T _____

He was born around 624 B.C. He was the first Greek scientist, mathematician, and philosopher to study natural forces and to form ideas about how nature works. He traveled widely to Egypt and the Near East. He formed geometric principles from studying the stars and the Earth and used these principles to calculate the heights of building and distances. He developed a theory that the Earth was flat and floated on water. He incorrectly concluded that earthquakes resulted from waves in the water. This made him one of the first thinkers to search for scientific explanations for events rather than relying on religion and the gods for meaning.

Answers—Fold under or cover before reproducing for students.

1. Archimedes
2. Empedocles
3. Eratosthenes
4. Euclid
5. Hipparchus
6. Hippocrates
7. Ptolemy
8. Pythagoras
9. Sappho
10. Sophocles
11. Strabon
12. Thales

The Pythagorean Theorem

Pythagoras was born around 584 B.C. on the Greek island of Samos. He became one of the greatest thinkers of his time. Although he is best known for his Pythagorean Theorem, geometry was only one of his areas of interest and writing. He believed that the Earth, heaven, and man were all joined together by astronomy, geometry, music, and religion.

Pythagoras traveled a great deal throughout Egypt, Babylonia, India, and Syria. His learning was influenced by the places and people that he met. He believed that all religions contained the same basic truth. He studied many different religions before formulating his theories. These theories became so well known that they even influenced the thought of later philosophers, such as Plato and Aristotle.

After his travels Pythagoras finally settled down in Croton, a Greek colony in southern Italy. There he established a school for both men and women that was almost like a religious order, requiring students to follow extremely strict rules. Those who attended were not allowed to eat meat or drink alcohol. They had to wear simple clothing and no shoes. The group was cut off from the rest of society so that they could develop pure bodies and minds.

Pythagoras believed that this purity could be achieved through scientific study. Mathematics was the most important subject taught there because Pythagoras believed that "all things are numbers," and he looked for mathematical relationships everywhere. His most influential theory was the Pythagorean Theorem. This theorem is used to find an unknown length of a side of a right triangle if given the length of the other two sides. It states: "In a right triangle, the square of the hypotenuse equals the sum of the squares of the other two sides." The hypotenuse is the side of the triangle opposite the right angle.

Pythagoras had learned the "3-4-5 triangle" from the Egyptians, who had the mathematical understanding of right angles long before the Greeks. The Egyptians used a long piece of rope with 12 knots tied an equal distance apart. Then they used the rope and stakes to form a right triangle. There would be three knots on one side, four knots on another, and five knots on the longest side. The Egyptians used the "3-4-5 triangle" and its calculations to measure land and create such wonders as the pyramids.

Yet, the Egyptians were only able to use geometry in a "hands-on" approach. Pythagoras and other Greeks took the development of geometry a step further. After they were able to see the problem visually, they could then understand how to measure and calculate theoretically or abstractly—in their minds. For example, Pythagoras first studied the side of a right triangle by visualizing the sides as three squares. He was then able to generalize the rule to all right triangles and create the mathematical equation $a^2 + b^2 = c^2$.

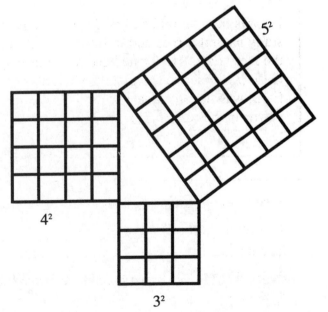

Eventually, people in Croton became suspicious of Pythagoras's school. There was unrest and a political uprising that killed many students. Pythagoras died in 506 B.C., but historians are uncertain whether he died in the uprising or escaped and died later.

Working with Right Triangles

The following activities will allow you to experience the Egyptian and Greek approaches to working with right triangles.

The Egyptian "Hands-On" Method

1. You will need a standard ruler, a 12-inch piece of string or yarn, a protractor, a piece of paper, a felt marker, three push-pins, and a surface into which you can push the pins, such as a bulletin board, piece of Styrofoam meat tray, or cardboard.

2. Beginning at one end of the string, mark with the felt pen at three inches and seven inches. You have now divided the string into the ratio 3:4:5.

3. Place the paper on your selected surface. Push a pin through the three-inch mark. Stretch the string in any direction on the paper and pin down at the seven-inch mark. Then bring the ends together to form a triangle and pin into position.

4. Trace the triangle you made onto the paper and then remove the pins and string. Use the protractor to measure the angle formed by the two shortest sides and record your results.

5. As an extension, repeat the process using a string 18 inches long marked at the 4½-inch and 10½-inch position or a string 9 inches long marked at the 2¼-inch and 5¼-inch position. What do you discover?

The Greek Pythagorean Theorem

After learning the 3-4-5 triangle from the Egyptians, Pythagoras was able to apply this knowledge to other theoretical examples. Pythagoras discovered that the square of the length of the hypotenuse on a right triangle is equal to the sum of the squares of the lengths of the other two sides. Therefore, to find the length of a missing side, use any of the following formulas:

$$a^2 + b^2 = c^2 \qquad c^2 - b^2 = a^2 \qquad c^2 - a^2 = b^2$$

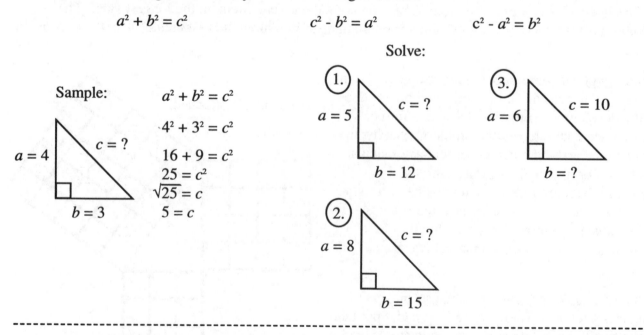

Solve:

Sample:

$$a^2 + b^2 = c^2$$
$$4^2 + 3^2 = c^2$$
$$16 + 9 = c^2$$
$$25 = c^2$$
$$\sqrt{25} = c$$
$$5 = c$$

Answers—Fold over or cover before reproducing for students.

1. $c = 13$ 2. $c = 17$ 3. $b = 8$

Magic Triangles and Squares

The Greeks continually observed patterns and relationships in nature to help explain concepts in such areas as geometry. Experiment with the activities below to discover some truths about lines, triangles, squares, and circles. Remember that all angle measurements are in degrees.

Materials: Gather scrap paper, tape, a pencil, a compass, and a protractor.

Problem #1: How are a triangle and a straight line alike?

1. Cut out a triangle of any shape and size and label the corners A, B, and C. Use the protractor to measure the three angles.

   A= _____ , B= _____ , C= _____ .

Add these together, and record the total: _____

2. Now tear off each of the corners, leaving the labels attached.

3. Put the corners together as shown.

4. Use the protractor to measure the straight line. Result: _____

5. Try this at least three more times and record your results. What happens each time? _____

Fact: The sum of the angles of a triangle equals _____ .

Fact: A straight line equals _____ .

Problem #2: How are a square and a circle alike?

1. Cut out a square of any size. Make sure it is a true square with four equal sides and four right angles.

2. Label the corners A, B, C, and D. Use the protractor to measure the four angles.

   A= _____ , B= _____ , C= _____ , D= _____ .

Add these together, and record the total: _____

3. Tear the square into fourths, leaving the corners intact and labels attached.

4. Put the corners together and tape them. Using the point where the corners meet as the center, use a compass to draw a circle.

5. Use the protractor to measure the circle. Result:

   _____

6. How are a square and a circle alike?

   _____

7. Try this at least three more times and record your results. What happens each time? _____

Fact: The sum of the angles of a square equals _____ .

Fact: A circle equals _____ .

Research Question: Are circles and straight lines also angles?

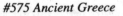

Living History—A Day in Ancient Greece

With the class, re-create a day in the life of the Ancient Greeks. Begin to plan for this day at least two weeks in advance. You may wish to team with another class or an entire grade level to share in this special day. Parents may also enjoy participating in all or some of the activities. After you have decided on a schedule of events, send home invitations with the basic schedule and proposed menu. Include a sign-up for food items and a copy of Greek Clothing and Music (page 147).

Suggested Activities to Schedule During the Day

1. Students bring their food items for the feast.

2. Students dress as Greeks (see pages 118 and 119 and 147).

3. The whole class or small groups perform a Greek drama. Students can dramatize one of the Moments in Time passages from the unit or write their own plays based on Greek myths. Other sources for appropriate dramas already in play format include *Teaching and Dramatizing Greek Myths* by Josephine Davidson (Teacher Ideas Press, 1989) and *Mythology I, Overhead Transparencies for Creative Dramatics* by Cheryl McGlocklin (Creative Teaching Press, 1989).

4. Do one of the suggested art projects from the unit: Minoan Pottery (pages 22–24), Make a Kaleidoscope Labyrinth (page 29), Cooperative Group Life Size Greek Gods and Poems (pages 86 and 87), Make a Greek Mask (page 96), Make a Hoplite Shield (page 102), Create a Greek Temple (page 114), Make a Plaster Relief Sculpture (page 116), Make a Clay Oil Lamp (page 117).

5. Prepare and eat an authentic Greek Feast. (Menu and recipe suggestions on pages 145 and 146). You may wish to "order-in" a feast from a local Greek restaurant for a nominal charge per student. Call ahead to see what they have to offer and their cost. They may even provide some Greek dancers for your feast!

6. Work off the lunch by teaching some simple Greek dance steps (page 148).

7. Watch a movie on Greek mythology. Two favorites are *Jason and the Argonauts* and *Clash of the Titans*.

8. Have students choose to work alone, in partners, or in groups to work on unit activities you may not have done or want to repeat. Refer to the pages listed:

    Perform Athenian courtroom drama (57–62)

    Use some trade science—Count Your Cargo (68 and 69)

    A Mycenaean Sunken Ship Investigation (74–76)

    Re-create Olympic competition with Estimation Pentathlon (91)

    Get philosophical with Socrates' Hot Seat (122)

    Debate which is the better city-state, Athens or Sparta (125–127)

    Play Strategy Skills, Macedonia/Thessaly/Peloponnesus (128)

    Play a research game on Greek achievements (138–140)

    Participate in a geometry activity: Magic Triangles and Squares (143)

A Day in Ancient Greece *(cont.)*

Greek Feast Menu and Recipes

WHITE AND RED GRAPE JUICE
ANTIPASTO SALAD BAR—LETTUCE,
CHERRY TOMATOES, HAM, SALAMI,
GREEK OLIVES, FETA CHEESE, RED
ONION, DRESSING
PITA BREAD
SPANIKOPITA (CHEESE OR
CHEESE/SPINACH PIES)

AVGOLEMONO SOUP (CHICKEN
BROTH AND RICE WITH EGG AND
LEMON)
BAKLAVA (HONEY-NUT PASTRY)
FRESH FRUIT SUCH AS GRAPES,
MELON, CHERRIES, AND PLUMS
FOR DESSERT

Spanikopita (cheese pies) Makes 8—10 pies

Filling:

1 pound crumbled feta cheese
3 beaten eggs

1 tablespoon olive oil
1 tablespoon chopped parsley

Pastry:

1-pound package of prepared phyllo dough (in freezer section of store) 1 cup melted butter and a pastry brush

These are VERY easy and students enjoy making these little burrito-like sandwiches. Remember to completely thaw out the dough according to the package directions and keep a moist cloth over the dough waiting to be used.

1. Mix all of the ingredients for the filling. Preheat the oven to 400° F.
2. Cover your work surface with wax paper. Place a sheet of dough on the wax paper and brush with the melted butter.
3. Place another sheet on top and brush it with melted butter.
4. Put about 2 tablespoons of filling at the narrow end of the dough and fold it like a burrito.
5. Place the folded dough seam side down on an oiled baking sheet. Brush with melted butter.
6. Continue to make cheese pies and place on the sheet until filling or dough is done.
7. Bake at 400° F for 25 to 30 minutes or until the pies are a light golden brown.
8. The spanikopita can be served cold or reheated and served warm.

Spanikopita (cheese and spinach pies) Makes 10–12 pies

Make these pies the same as the ones above but use the following ingredients for the filling:

4 eggs
1/2 pound of crumbled feta cheese
1 bunch of green onion, chopped
1/4 cup of parsley, chopped

1/4 cup of fresh dill, chopped or 1 tablespoon of dried dill
2 packages of frozen chopped spinach that has been defrosted and squeezed dry

A Day in Ancient Greece *(cont.)*

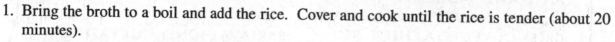

Avgolemono Soup Serves 6–8 people

64 ounces (8 cups) of chicken broth
½ cup uncooked rice
4 eggs beaten
Juice of 2 lemons

1. Bring the broth to a boil and add the rice. Cover and cook until the rice is tender (about 20 minutes).
2. Remove the broth and rice from the heat.
3. Mix the eggs and lemon juice together. Then add two cups of the soup to the eggs and juice. Beat constantly until well mixed.
4. Add the diluted egg-lemon juice mixture to the rest of the soup, beating constantly.
5. Heat the soup but do not let it boil or it will curdle.

Baklava (honey and nut pastry) Makes 24 pieces

Filling:

2 cups chopped pecans
½ sugar
¼ cup butter
½ teaspoon of cinnamon
½ teaspoon of ground cloves

Pastry:

1 package prepared phyllo dough (in freezer section of store)
½ cup melted butter and a brush
1 cup heated light Karo syrup or honey

Baklava is very easy to make as long as you thaw out the phyllo dough according to the package directions and keep a moist towel over the dough waiting to be used.

1. Combine all of the ingredients for the filling. Preheat oven to 300 F°.
2. On a greased baking sheet with sides, place one sheet of dough. Brush it with melted butter.
3. Put another sheet on top and brush with melted butter. Continue this process until you have seven layers of dough.
4. Spread the sugar-nut mixture onto the layers of dough.
5. Place a sheet of dough on top and brush with butter. Continue this process until you have Seven layers of dough on top of the sugar-nut mixture.
7. Cut into 24 squares and then bake at 300 F° for about 30 minutes or until golden brown.
8. Remove from the oven and pour on the heated syrup or honey while the tray is still hot.
9. Let the pastry cool and then cover and refrigerate.
10. Serve at room temperature.

146

A Day in Ancient Greece *(cont.)*

Greek Clothing and Music

The Greeks loved to dress up and give a symposium party! Use the directions throughout the unit to make a costume for your Living History Day.

Hair—Greek men did not do anything special to their hair. Occasionally they would wear a headband of cloth or gold cord. Greek women usually wore a headband or would curl their hair up in elaborate folds on top of their heads. Women wore decorative hair combs, barrettes, and fresh flowers in their hair. Remember, the Athenians placed great value on their women looking graceful and beautiful.

Make-up and Fragrance—The Greeks took great care of their bodies with scented oils and lotions. Women may have worn a little make-up on their eyes, cheeks, and lips— much as we do today. The idea is to look naturally beautiful and not "made-up," so use make-up sparingly.

Jewelry—Wealthy Greeks wore fashionable brooches, pins, rings, necklaces, and bracelets to adorn their chitons or peplos. They did not flaunt their wealth, so do not make the jewelry overwhelming.

Clothing—Review the directions for making a simple chiton or peplos (pages 118–119). Use white or brightly colored fabric. You may wish to decorate the edge of the fabric in Greek designs, using fabric paints or permanent markers.

Footwear—Any type of sandal will do. You may want to use a string, piece of yarn, or strap of leather to make a tie that crisscrosses and wraps up your leg. This style was especially prominent for soldiers and heroes wearing the shorter chitons.

Music—The Greeks believed music had magical powers to heal sickness, purify the body and mind, and work miracles in nature. The main function of music was to accompany poetry, drama, or dance. Lyres and kitharas were harp and guitar-type instruments with five to seven strings. Aulos were double-piped reed instruments with a shrill, piercing tone. Music using these instruments was used for weddings and funerals, banquets and parties, harvests and other types of work, and for religious purposes.

Music festivals and competitions became quite popular after the 5th century B.C. The Greeks put on great competitions much like the Olympics or Drama Festival to Dionysus whereby competitors would come from regions far from Greece to participate. To the Greeks, music was also a part of a gentleman's education. Plato believed music perfected the soul like gymnastics built the body. Pythagoras discovered that music could be represented in mathematical terms of ratio, thus making music a "serious" subject like science and astronomy. The word "music" comes from the Greek word "muse." The muses were nine sister goddesses who presided over certain arts and sciences. Check with a local music store for traditional Greek folk music. Explain that you will be using the music for dancing. If you cannot find a tape you like, try calling a local Greek restaurant—they may have music they play while customers dine.

A Day in Ancient Greece *(cont.)*

Greek Dance Steps

Make sure you have a large open space for teaching dancing where the music can also be heard. The cafeteria or multipurpose room with a sound system is ideal so that you can describe directions to the group using a microphone, and later play the music over the speakers. It is also helpful to teach a small group of students ahead of time so that they can demonstrate and teach the others while you describe the steps.

1. Review rules for participating in the group dancing. Have the students stand apart from each other with their arms outstretched. Without the music, describe and demonstrate the steps below. Have students try the steps by themselves. When students can do the steps, have them make a large circle by placing their hands on the shoulders of the people next to them. Tell them not to get too close to each other or they may fall. Without playing the music, call out the directions and see that they can do the steps. Remind students to try to make the movements all together at the same time. After practicing a few times, turn on the music, find the beat, and do the dance steps to the pace of the music. You may want to still call out directions.

Variations:

- Have the girls make one circle and the boys make another circle. Let them compete to see who can do the best dancing.

- Make a large circle around a smaller circle in the middle and have the two circles dance in opposite directions.

- Instead of making a closed circle, have one person be the leader and wind the circle around like a big coil towards the inside. Stop when there is no more room to dance.

The Dance Steps: There are just four moves that repeat over and over. It is best if you call out the directions for each move rather than counting a beat. "Over in front, behind and back, point, point— Over in front, behind and back, point, point, etc."

Step 1: "Over—in Front": Begin with your feet apart and arms outstretched. You will be moving to the left, so make sure you have plenty of room. Try to keep your upper torso always facing forward while you twist and bend at your waist and knees. Cross your right foot over in front of your left foot twisting and bending down with your knees. Then step your left foot back out so that your feet are spread apart again.

Step 2: "Behind—and Back": This time cross your right foot behind your left foot twisting and bending down with your knees. Then step your left foot back out so that your feet are spread apart again.

Step 3: "Point": Point your right foot to the left with your right foot.

Step 4: "Point": Point your left foot to the right.

Step 4   Step 3   Step 2   Step 1

Ancient Greece—Assessment

Answer all questions with complete and well-elaborated sentences. Complete other items by following the directions in the given section.

Geography

1. Describe the geography of Ancient Greece. _____

2. How did these geographical features influence farming, trade, mythology, and the development of individual city-states? _____

3. Label the map below with the following:

   Aegean Sea

   Asia Minor

   Peloponnesian Peninsula

   Crete

   Ionian Sea

   Mediterranean Sea

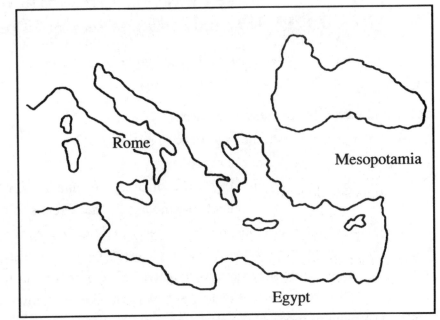

Government

4. Describe the changes that occurred in Athenian government by explaining each type of government and why it failed.

   Monarchy— _____

   Tyranny— _____

   Oligarchy— _____

   Democracy— _____

5. Describe how these features of Greek democracy are similar to or different from democracy today:

   Citizenship— _____

   Voting— _____

   Courts— _____

Ancient Greece—Assessment *(cont.)*

Economy, Trade, and Transportation

Fill in the blanks with correct terms.

6. The Greeks did not have much good soil for growing grain, so they would _____ grain from other places around the Mediterranean.

7. Olive products were in abundant supply. This is why olives and olive oil were two leading _____ of Greece.

8. Greek merchants originally acquired goods by_____ or trading goods for other goods. Later, _____ were developed from gold and silver, which allowed merchants to buy and sell any products freely.

9. Triremes were Greek _____ ships that were narrow and swift with three rows of oarsmen. They were faster than the wide-bodied merchant ships used to transport goods.

Religion

Circle the letter for the correct answer.

10. The Greeks worshipped their gods because. . . .
    a. they were perfect in every way.
    b. they believed that they had control over events in their lives.
    c. they provided excellent role models for the Greeks to follow.

11. Which of the following was NOT a way that the Greeks worshipped the gods?
    a. They participated at the Olympics and made animal sacrifices at temples.
    b. They wrote plays and participated at the drama festivals.
    c. They built churches and went every Sunday with large groups of Greeks.

12. The main purpose of Greek mythology was to. . . .
    a. help explain the world around them, as well as to learn about the gods.
    b. entertain children at the drama festivals.
    c. create fantasy images of faraway places so that the Greeks would fear travel.

13. Which statement is true for BOTH drama today and in Ancient Greece?
    a. All actors are male.
    b. Story plots usually help the audience learn important lessons.
    c. The chorus sings and dances in an area known as the orchestra.

Match each god/goddess to the appropriate description. Place the correct letter on the line:

___14. Zeus   a. Goddess of love and beauty

___15. Poseidon   b. King of the gods, controller of the skies

___16. Hades   c. God of light, truth, healing, archery, and music

___17. Athena   d. God of the Underworld, death, and greed

___18. Aphrodite   e. Goddess of wisdom, war, arts, and weaving

___19. Apollo   f. God of the seas

___20. Hera   g. Queen of the gods, goddess of marriage

Ancient Greece—Assessment *(cont.)*

Athens and Sparta

Write **A** if the statement describes Athens and **S** if the statement describes Sparta. For questions 35 and 36 write your answers on the back of this page.

21. Run by democracy. _____

22. Male landowners were the only citizens. _____

23. Emphasis was on strong military power and harsh living conditions. _____

24. Men and women were considered citizens. _____

25. Women and girls participated in athletic contests. _____

26. Run by an oligarchy. _____

27. The navy was their strongest weapon. _____

28. Emphasis was on the development and beauty of the mind, body, and soul. _____

29. Boys were raised in barracks by other male soldiers. _____

30. Male citizens were farmers, traders, merchants, politicians, etc. _____

31. Their strength was in their fearless foot soldiers and land army. _____

32. Boys were educated at schools or by fathers to learn a trade. _____

33. Women and girls did not participate in most public life. _____

34. The slaves did all of the farming. _____

35. What was the Persian War? Why was it fought? Who won and what did it cause?

36. What was the Peloponesian War? Why was it fought? Who won and what did it cause?

Contributions

Describe the accomplishments of these famous Greeks:

37. Pericles_____

38. Socrates _____

39. Alexander the Great_____

40. The Greeks showed great artistic skill and created unique art forms. If you were at a museum, how would you know the following were Greek? What distinguishing features do they have?

    Greek Sculpture _____

    Greek Pottery _____

    Greek Architecture_____

41. Name at least three other lasting contributions or achievements made by the Greeks.

42. What aspects of life in Ancient Greece would you like to incorporate into your life today? What valuable lessons have you learned by studying these people?

Ancient Greece Assessment—Key

Geography

1. The physical geography includes many mountains on the mainland and the islands off the coasts. A large peninsula extends into the surrounding seas.

2. The mountains and islands made it difficult for there to be one united country with one type of government. Since most regions were cut off from one another, they developed their own city-states and needed to trade with other regions. The mountains also made it difficult to farm, so they needed to import grain. Since people were isolated and there were hundreds of little islands in the areas, many stories were told by traders and travelers about mythological places.

3. Refer to a map of the region.

Government

4. A monarchy is run by one king with ultimate control. He is not elected but born into the position. It failed because kings needed to rely on other wealthy land owners for protection who eventually wanted some of the power. An oligarchy formed in which a small group of wealthy people had power over the whole. Eventually the oligarchy failed because the region was unable to provide enough food for its people. People became upset and put a new leader into power by force. A tyranny developed, which is a government run by one leader who gained power by force. Some tyrants were good, but others were bad. Eventually, the tyrants were thrown out and Athens developed a democracy, which shared the decision-making among the people regardless of wealth.

5. Citizenship—only male land owners in Athens. Cannot gain citizenship if female or foreign.

   Voting—only male citizens could vote in Athens.

   Courts—only male citizens allowed to speak or participate in justice. All had rights but had to be represented by a male citizen. Courts were made up of hundreds of jurors as opposed to only 12 today.

Economy, Trade, and Transportation

6. import
7. exports
8. barter, coins
9. war

Religion

10. b
11. c
12. a
13. b
14. b
15. f
16. d
17. e
18. a
19. c
20. g

Athens and Sparta

21. A
22. A
23. S
24. S
25. S
26. S
27. A
28. A
29. S
30. A
31. S
32. A
33. A
34. S

35. The Persian War was a war in which Athens and Sparta fought together against Persia. It was fought because Persia took revenge against Athens for defending a Greek colony in Asia Minor. Eventually the Greeks won and the victory began the Golden Age of Athens.

36. The Peloponnesian War was a civil war between Athens and Sparta. It was fought because Sparta felt Athens was gaining too much power over other city-states. Athens refused to give up control. Sparta eventually won, ending the Golden Age of Athens.

Contributions

37. Pericles—a famous Athenian statesman who brought Athens to its peak of power by strengthening its walls and navy, building and improving the beauty of Athens, and making policies to spread democracy and improve participation in government.

38. Socrates—a famous philosopher who attempted to educate others by asking probing questions and making them think for themselves. He was forced to commit suicide when he was charged with corrupting the youth of Athens.

39. Alexander—Macedonian raised and educated in Greece who became the leader of the largest Greek Empire ever known. Known for spreading Greek knowledge and culture while adopting native ways.

40. Sculpture is lifelike and made from bronze or marble. Often shows nude athletes, gods/goddesses, or typical Greek culture and dress. Pottery is black and terracotta in a variety of shapes. The surface is etched to show typical Greek lifestyle, mythology, and designs. Architecture generally shows columns, friezes, and relief carvings.

41. and 42. Accept reasonable answers.

Literature Connection Planning Guide

Section 1—Hercules

Comprehension Questions and Activities
Descriptive Writing
Letter from Iolaus—written language
The 12 Labors of Hercules—small group research, class drama or making class book
Prometheus on Trial—small group drama
Make an Adventure Map—geography skills

Section 2—Perseus

Comprehension Questions and Activities
Sequence of Events and Summary
Using Exaggeration—written language
Greek Fate—The Myth-Adventures of Perseus

Section 3—Theseus

Comprehension Questions and Activities
Cultural Clues
Create *The Greek Gazette*—classroom magazine
Theseus Dramas
Letter to King Aegeus—written language

Section 4—Orpheus

Comprehension Questions and Activities
Who Is More Powerful?—debate and persuasive writing
Take My Advice—written language
Comparing Myths—small group research and drama
Superhuman You—written or oral language

Section 5—Meleager

Comprehension Questions and Activities
Meleager Muses—descriptive writing

Section 6—Jason and the Argonauts

Comprehension Questions and Activities
Jason's Travel Log—written language
A Hero for Today—written or oral language
Make a Hero Adventure Mural—art

Using Literature

The literature lessons are arranged so that they correspond to sections of the book. Below is a suggested format for each section of the book:

Prereading Activity—discuss past chapters, predict future events, and connect the story to other classroom activities.

Read the Section—choose from a variety of reading stratagies for each section (page 155).

Comprehension Activity—see the questions and activities listed for each section, as well as the strategies for comprehension activity (page 155).

Written Language Activity

Hands-On Activity

Preparing for Teaching the Literature Lessons

1. Students can make a Literature Journal by stapling writing paper into construction paper covers before starting the lessons. This allows them to keep a record of their responses to comprehension questions, activities, key words, and their thoughts and feelings about the story as they read it. Have the students decorate the front covers with the title of the book, their names, and appropriate illustrations.

2. Review the story and make notes in your copy of the book. This allows you to easily find key words, descriptions, figurative language, and sections covered by the comprehension questions and activities.

3. Review the different lessons for the Literature Unit. Plan to gather the materials you need ahead of time. Decide how much time you want to schedule for each of the activities.

4. This particular book did not seem to warrant vocabulary lists for each reading section. However, you may want students to keep a list of key terms or words that are unfamiliar to them in their Literature Journals to discuss as a class.

Reading and Comprehension Strategies

Choose from among these reading techniques to introduce each story section. Depending upon the reading levels in your classroom, you may want to incorporate more than one strategy at a time.

- **Round Robin Reading**—Have students orally read in groups, taking turns around the table.

- **Popcorn Reading**—Read orally as a class allowing students to call on other students. Give an incentive for everyone to follow along, such as points for being in the right place when called upon.

- **Partner Reading**—Have students pair up and read silently or orally to each other.

- **Teacher Reading**—Read aloud the section or part of the section to the class.

- **Silent Reading**—Have students read the section silently on their own.

To help your students better understand each story section, use the comprehension questions listed for each section and choose from among these comprehension techniques.

- **Written Response**—Have students answer some or all of the questions, using complete sentences, in their Literature Journals. Choose whether students will work independently, with partners, or in small groups. Discuss responses together as a class when completed.

- **Comprehension Hot Seat**—Have one student come to the front of the class to portray one of the characters from the book. Have the rest of the students ask appropriate questions from the list along with questions of their own. The student in the hot seat should respond to the question appropriately as the story character. Have students think carefully about how the character would talk, feel, move, etc. Evaluate the student's ability to respond correctly, based on his or her assumed identity. Have students take turns being other story characters in the hot seat.

- **Comprehension Hide-And-Seek**—Split the class into four groups. Give each group a different color of index cards. Tell them to make two piles. Have students write the questions on one pile of index cards and answers on another. Have each group hide their cards for another group to find. Once the group has found all of the necessary cards they should match the questions with the correct answers. Have each group evaluate the correctness of the responses on the cards.

- **Writing Dialogues**—Have students write dialogues between characters from the story, answering one or more of the questions. Invite volunteers to read their dialogues to the class.

- **Comprehension Battle**—Divide the class into cooperative groups and assign each person in the group a number from 1–4. Give each group pieces of scratch paper to write their answers. Tell them to write their group's "name" at the top of each piece. Then, give each question from the list a point value and play the game. Read a question aloud and disclose the point value. Allow about one minute for the groups to quietly discuss their answer. Call "time" and then tell the number of the person who is to write the response on the paper (1–4). There is to be no talking while the person is writing or the team is disqualified. Allow them 1–2 minutes to write and WALK the answer up to you. The paper must be in your hands before the time is up or the team receives no points. Read the answers and award all or partial points based on their answers. Continue in this manner assigning writers in a random order so that all students must participate on each question.

Background Information

About the Authors: Mollie McLean and Anne Wiseman were teachers together in Baltimore, Maryland. They noticed that there was a scarcity of interesting and readable books available for older children. So they joined together to write *Adventures of the Greek Heroes*, their first book.

Book Summary: This book contains a collection of stories that have been retold throughout the centuries about heroic men who are both clever and brave. Hercules comes to the rescue of Prometheus, a mortal who has been chained to a rock as his punishment for stealing fire from the gods. Angered at his escape, the gods force Hercules into the bondage of a wicked king, who makes Hercules perform 12 seemingly impossible tasks. Three of these are included in this book. Then Hercules battles Death to save the life of a woman who has offered her life so that her husband could live.

In the story of Perseus, a king is warned that his grandson will eventually kill him. So when his daughter has the child, he casts them away to another kingdom. There a jealous king sends Perseus out to slay Medusa, a monster who turns mortals to stone with one evil glance. Perseus succeeds with the help of the gods and through his own cunning and bravery. He carries Medusa's head back and uses it to kill the giant Atlas and a terrible sea monster who is about to devour a beautiful woman. He marries the beautiful woman and returns to his grandfather's kingdom to complete the circle of fate by accidentally killing him with a heavy rock.

The king of Athens fathers a son whom he leaves with the child's mother when he returns to Athens. When Theseus, the son, is older he goes to Athens to claim his place on the throne. On his journey he encounters three wicked villains who attempt to destroy him. Theseus outwits them, learning valuable life lessons. Theseus sails to Crete with a boatload of victims to be sacrificed to the Minotaur, in hopes of slaying the beast. With help from the princess of Crete, Theseus succeeds and sails back to Athens. The princess is abandoned on a nearby island, and Theseus forgets to hoist the white sails of victory as he enters the harbor. Thinking his son has been killed, the king commits suicide by leaping into the ocean.

Orpheus is the most gifted musician in all of Greece. All people and nature fall under the spell of his singing and lyre. He marries a lovely girl who is one day killed by a snake. Orpheus cannot live without her and decides to make the dangerous journey to the Underworld and bring her back. The god Pluto, who rules the Underworld, is lured by the beautiful music of Orpheus and agrees to let his wife return. Orpheus is warned not to look behind him as he leads her from the Underworld, but he cannot resist and loses his wife forever.

A mother is warned that her baby son, Meleager, will die as soon as a log in the hearth in burned up. To save her son, she puts out the fire and hides the log. Meleager grows up to become strong and wise. However, his father neglects to honor the goddess Diana, and she retaliates by sending a giant boar to ravage the forests. With the help of a huntress, Meleager kills the boar and his two evil uncles. His mother misunderstands the deed and throws the hidden log back on the fire, thus committing Meleager to his death.

Jason is raised by a wise Centaur. The boy hears about the Golden Fleece, the skin of a magic sheep whose wool is pure gold. Determined to seek this prize, Jason sends for all young heroes to join him on his quest. Calling themselves the Argonauts, they sail off in search of the Golden Fleece and encounter many troubles. Once they arrive at their destination, the king assigns them two impossible tasks. Jason and his men succeed with the help of the king's daughter. Jason then steals the Golden Fleece and escapes with the king's daughter.

Before Reading the Book

Before you begin reading *Adventures of the Greek Heroes* with your students, do some prereading activities to stimulate their interest and enhance their comprehension.

Mapping the Heroes—The stories describe real and make-believe places in Greece. Have students refer to map of Greece to locate key places such as Athens, Olympia, and Crete. Note the bodies of water surrounding Greece and how they are referred to in the literature. Refer back to the Geography section of this unit (pages 10-15) for ideas on making maps.

Elements of Mythology—Discuss the use of mythology in all cultures. Remind students that myths were originally handed down by word of mouth. You may wish to review pages 35–43 of this unit about Homer, *The Iliad*, and the importance of Greek storytelling in their culture. You can also refer to page 88 for directions on how students can write their own myths. Review with students elements usually found in Greek myths and have them record these elements in their journals:

1. Myths may have been written to explain a natural phenomena, such as why the sun rises, etc.

2. They usually contain good and evil royalty, such as kings, princesses, etc.

3. It is common for sons to be raised by someone other than their parents.

4. Myths contain imaginative creatures, people, and animals displaying unusual qualities.

5. There is often the use of magic to undermine the hero or move the plot along.

6. The gods play a significant role in helping or hindering the main characters.

7. The "good" characters of the story all show similar characteristics—young, handsome, clever, etc.

8. Myths often rely on the belief in fate, which cannot be changed regardless of the character's actions.

As you read each story, note which elements were used by writing the name of the story next to the element. Which elements seems to be used most often?

Charting the Heroes—Ask students to name people they would consider to be heroes. Have them give reasons for their choices and list these characteristics on the board. Tell them that they will be reading about men whom the Greeks considered heroes. Have them make a large chart in their journals to list the heroes, their adventures, and their characteristics to see if the storybook heroes match their modern-day definition of a hero. Discuss their findings after each story section.

What's In a Name?—Throughout this book the gods provide help and obstacles to the main characters. In many cases the Roman name for the god has been used. Keep a list of the gods on the board as they appear in the literature. Write down their Greek name, their Roman name, and their actions in the story. You may refer to page 85 of this unit for an overview of the Greek gods.

The Pursuit of Excellence—Read aloud the introduction to the book. Discuss with students the importance of excellence and achievement in Greek culture. Ask students if they think we value excellence and achievement today in the same way. Then divide the class into four debating teams and have them prepare arguments for two different debates:

Debate #1: We are/are not as committed to physical excellence as the Ancient Greeks.

Debate #2: We are/are not as committed to intellectual excellence as the Ancient Greeks.

Encourage students to use as much information as possible gained from this unit. Refer to page 57 for directions on leading a debate.

Section 1—Hercules

Comprehension Questions

1. Name three gods from the first story and their gifts to man. *(Diana—the moon, Apollo—the sun, Neptune—the sea, Vulcan—fire)*

2. Do you think Prometheus would have done his deed if he knew of the possible punishment? Why or why not? *(Accept reasonable answers.)*

3. List the labors of Hercules from the second story. How are the labors similar? How are they different? *(Kill the lion of Nemea and bring back its skin, kill the Lernean Hydra, and bring back the cattle of Geryon. All of the stories have fierce monsters with unusual qualities. In each story Hercules uses his great strength and weapons to kill them. The last story uses magic and the gods help/hinder Hercules along the way.)*

4. Why was king Admetus both happy and sad at the beginning of the story? *(He is happy because he is in love, but sad because he thinks he can never fulfill her father's demands and marry her.)*

5. Why wouldn't anyone die for the king? *(They were all afraid to die in sickness.)*

6. Why do you think Hercules took on the battle with Death? *(King Admetus was good and kind. He took care of Hercules when he came to visit, never once thinking of his own sorrow. Accept any other reasonable answers.)*

Comprehension Activities

1. Have students use the chart they made in their Literature Journal to fill in the information for Hercules describing his adventures and character traits. Discuss together as a class.

2. Have students locate examples of elements of Greek mythology in these stories and record their findings in their journals. Discuss together as a class.

3. Distribute construction paper and have students draw a picture of Hercules based on the description by Prometheus and elsewhere. Have students write the sentences or phrases from the book that give descriptions and the page numbers where they were found. Evaluate the pictures based on how close they relate to the passage and not the book's illustrations.

4. Have students compare the two kings, King Eurystheus and King Admetus, from the Hercules stories by drawing a Venn Diagram. Discuss their conclusions as a class.

5. Divide the class into groups and have each group perform a character analysis on one of the main characters from the stories: Hercules, Prometheus, King Eurystheus, King Admetus, Alcestis, Apollo, and Death. Have them record character traits and evidence from the story that reflect these traits. Then have them use that information to write similes and metaphors to describe their characters. Combine the similes and metaphors to make a poem. Share the poems and display them in the classroom. Have each group add an illustration of their character.

Descriptive Writing

Find each event in the second story about Hercules. Pretend that you are the editor of this book and have decided to elaborate on each of these scenes. Use a variety of descriptive language devices to make each scene more sensory and exciting. Try to use similes, metaphors, personification, and other types of figurative language.

1. Apollo arrives with the chariot _____

   _____

   _____

   _____

2. How sick King Admetus OR Alcestis looked _____

   _____

   _____

   _____

3. The funeral for Alcestis _____

   _____

   _____

   _____

4. The battle between Hercules and Death _____

   _____

   _____

   _____

5. The reunion of Admetus and Alcestis _____

   _____

   _____

   _____

Letter From Iolaus

Have students pretend that they are Iolaus helping Hercules with his labors. Have each write a letter home to their father describing their adventure. Make sure they use specific details from the story to describe events and their feelings. Evaluate the letters based on content and proper letter format. Choose a few examples to share with the class.

The 12 Labors of Hercules

Have a group of students research to find a description of the 12 labors of Hercules. Divide the class into 9 groups and assign each group one of the labors not described in the literature connection book. Have each group write and act out a brief drama to perform for the rest of the class describing the labor. Or have each group write about and illustrate their labor and combine them in a class book. Discuss why students think the authors chose the three labors they did to include in their book.

Prometheus on Trial

In giving fire to the earth-dwellers, Prometheus defied Zeus and was punished. Pretend that rather than Prometheus receiving a physical punishment directly, Zeus had filed charges against him in the assembly. Choose a small group of capable students to reenact the trial of Prometheus. They will need a timer, two token counters, "guilty" and "not guilty" tokens for each audience member, and a person to play each of the following parts: the statesman chosen to run the trial, Zeus, a supporter of Zeus, Prometheus, and a supporter for Prometheus.

Refer to page 57 of this unit to help set up the courtroom drama. Allow time for students to prepare their case and gather needed props. On the day of the trial, have the group present their drama and let the audience cast their votes. Discuss the outcomes of the trial. Was the verdict similar or different than the punishment in the myth? How did constructing a trial change the situation?

Make an Adventure Map

There are many geographical locations described in the stories about Hercules. Reproduce a map of the entire Mediterranean area and its surrounding countries. Have students locate and label places mentioned throughout the passages. Have students draw an adventure route to show the path Hercules took on his different journeys. Check to make sure students have made a legend or key for their map, as well as a compass rose.

Section 2—Perseus

Comprehension Questions

1. Why must the king give up his daughter? What does this tell you about Greek superstition? *(It was told in the stars that his grandson would eventually kill him; therefore, he had to do what he could to prevent this from happening. The Greeks relied heavily on premonitions and believed in what oracles or magicians told them.)*

2. Why do you think the king did not kill his daughter and her son himself? *(Accept reasonable answers.)*

3. Why does the king send Perseus to kill Medusa? *(Perseus has grown strong. The king is afraid he might want to take over his kingdom, so he sends him on a deadly mission to get rid of him.)*

4. How can the helmet and shoes help kill Medusa? The knife and shield? *(The helmet makes him invisible and the shoes make him fly. The knife was able to cut off Medusa's head, and the shield he used as a mirror to see her without turning to stone.)*

5. Why did Perseus turn Atlas to stone? How did he accomplish this? Do you think he was justified in his actions? Why or why not? *(He killed him in self-defense by holding up the head of Medusa. Accept reasonable answers for the last portions.)*

6. What did Perseus want as his reward for killing the sea monster? Do you think this was an adequate award? Why or why not? *(He wanted the beautiful Andromeda for his wife. Accept reasonable answers for the last portions.)*

7. Why do you think the gods keep in touch with Perseus throughout the story? *(Accept reasonable answers.)*

8. In the end, why does Perseus kill his grandfather? *(It was fate, and the Greeks believed that this was stronger than the power of man.)*

Comprehension Activities

1. Have students use the chart in their Literature Journals to fill in the information for Perseus, describing his adventures and character traits. Discuss their findings as a class.

2. Have students locate examples of elements of Greek mythology in this story and record their findings in their journals. Discuss their conclusions as a class.

3. Have each student make a character web showing the different characters from the story and how they relate to one another. They can put the names in circles and connect them with lines. On or near the lines they can write the relationship between the characters. Have students include the following characters: Perseus, Danae, Zeus, King Acrisius, Dion, the fisherman, the king who raised Perseus, The Graeae Sisters, Medusa, Mercury, Minerva, Atlas, Andromeda, and Phineus.

4. Debate whether cunning and deceit are proper character traits for a hero. For example, Perseus deceives the Graeae sisters to steal their eye and uses trickery to avoid looking directly at Medusa. Have students defend their points of view orally or in writing.

Sequence of Events Summary

Put the following events in order. Then use these events to help you write a summary of the story.

_____   Perseus turns Phineus to stone.

_____   Danae and Perseus are sent out to sea where a fisherman finds them.

_____   Perseus rescues Danae from the dungeon.

_____   Perseus steals the Graeae Sisters' eye.

_____   Perseus kills Medusa.

_____   Dion came to warn the king of Perseus.

_____   Perseus turns Atlas to stone.

_____   The king sends Perseus to kill Medusa.

_____   Perseus saves Andromeda from the sea monster.

_____   Danae was locked in the dungeon and was visited by Zeus.
                   They married and had Perseus.

_____   Perseus is helped by the gods.

_____   Perseus kills his grandfather with a rock.

Summary

_____

_____

_____

_____

_____

_____

_____

_____

Using Exaggeration

In the story about Perseus, the authors use exaggeration to describe people, places, and events.

For example: ". . .more herds of sheep and oxen than there are stars in the sky."

"He could run faster than the king's best horse."

Use this method of figurative language to write descriptive sentences of these people, places, and events from the story.

1. The dungeon _____

_____

2. Floating out to sea _____

_____

3. Medusa_____

_____

4. Atlas_____

_____

5. Andromeda_____

_____

6. The golden apples and garden of Atlas _____

_____

7. The battle with the sea monster_____

_____

8. The new kingdom of Perseus_____

_____

Greek Fate

Discuss the Greek concept of fate and man's powerlessness to overcome what is destined to happen. Remind students that the old king does not blame Perseus for his death, for he understands that it was his fate. Find other examples throughout the book that rely on fate to further the plot. Examples include Atlas' death and Prometheus' rescue by Hercules. Ask students if they agree or disagree with this attitude. If you wish, schedule a classroom debate to discuss the issue further.

Distribute paper and have students make a list of events in their lives and futures that they DO have control over. Items should include their education, hobbies, and career goals, as well as their personal relationships with friends and family. Then have them make a list of events that they DO NOT have control over. These items might include where they live, their family members, and their physical features. Have them compare the two lists. Which list is the longest? Discuss ways in which students can help make their future go in the direction they desire, rather than accepting that fate will determine it for them. Actions include working hard in school, following rules and laws, choosing the right friends, avoiding drugs, setting goals, etc. Remind students that they ALWAYS have choices but that it is up to them to make the right choices to determine their future.

The Myth-Adventures of Perseus

Have students work in partners to write more adventures of Perseus and combine them to make a classroom novel. Begin by listing the main events or scenes from the stories. Then choose places in the story where new adventures could be inserted. Have some partners rewrite the book sections in more detail while keeping true to the plot. Have other partners write new and exciting adventures to insert. Encourage students to use the elements of myths and other Greek features such as dress, food, places, etc.

Once the compositions are completed, help students write transitional sentences to help the novel fit together. Have partners complete a final draft with colorful illustrations. Combine the book and read it as a class. Share the book with other classes.

Scenes for the Myth-Adventures of Perseus

1. Book introduction—King and fate, daughter in dungeon, marry Zeus, birth of Perseus.
2. Book scene—send daughter and son out to sea, found by fisherman, raised by cruel king.
3. New scene from Perseus's childhood showing his strength and intellect.
4. Book scene—Perseus sent on mission by king, meet Graeae sisters.
5. New adventure with the helmet and sandals, this time deep in the forest.
6. New adventure where Perseus gets the knife and shield from the gods and heads for Medusa.
7. Book scene—killing of Medusa.
8. New adventure with Medusa's head, this time on an island.
9. New adventure in Egypt, but don't use Medusa's head to overcome evil, head to Atlas.
10. Book scene—killing of Atlas at garden.
11. New adventure while flying.
12. Book scene—killing of sea monster for Andromeda, killing of Phineus, head home.
13. New adventure—something happens to Andromeda on way home to mother and cruel king.
14. Book scene—find mother in dungeon, kill cruel king.
15. New adventure with Andromeda and mother on way to original kingdom.
16. Book scene—arrive back home, accidentally kill king with stone, fate.

Section 3—Theseus

Comprehension Questions

1. Based on what Theseus was taught as a youth, what different qualities did the Greeks teach their sons? *(It was important to be strong, wise, well-read, happy and fun-loving, brave in battle, and humble.)*

2. Theseus kills three men on his way to Athens. What do you think justifies his actions? *(Accept reasonable answers.)*

3. Why didn't the king recognize his son? What kept him from poisoning him with the potion from Medea the witch? *(He was under a spell by Medea. When Theseus pulled out the sword and sandals it seemed to break the spell and the king knocked away the poison.)*

4. Do you think it was right for Ariadne to defy her father and help Theseus? Why or why not? *(Accept reasonable answers.)*

5. Why did King Aegeus throw himself off the cliff? Do you feel this was necessary for the plot? *(He killed himself out of grief for his son, whom he thought was dead. Accept reasonable answers for the other portion.)*

Comprehension Activities

1. Have students use the chart in their Literature Journals to record information for Theseus, describing his adventures and characters traits. Discuss as a class.

2. Have students locate examples of elements of Greek mythology in this story and record their findings in their journals. Discuss their conclusions as a class.

3. Draw a Venn diagram like the one shown to compare Hercules, Perseus, and Theseus. How are the heroes like or different? Discuss childhood, education, adventures, relationship with the gods, and outcomes of their adventures.

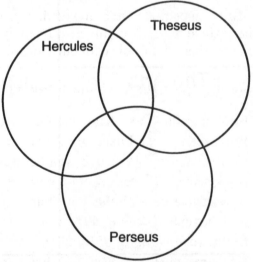

4. Have students find the main scenes from the story and write an outline of the plot. Roman numerals should be used for the main events and letters for the supporting details. Check outlines for correct sequence of events, understanding of main events, and proper outline format.

5. Have students work in small groups to discuss what kind of king Theseus would have become. Remind groups to base their predictions upon clues from the story. Include his family life, his education, his life experiences, his adventures in Athens, and other clues about his personality and capabilities. Have a volunteer from each group describe their predictions.

6. Refer to the Minoan section of this unit (pages 25–28) for other activities regarding the story of Theseus and the Minotaur.

Cultural Clues

The literature and mythology from a civilization give us many clues about their culture and values. Look at the following categories. Using the stories you have read so far, write information you have learned about the Greeks for each category. Include the name of the story where you find the information.

Family Life	Men's Roles	Women's Roles
Economy/Trade	**Government** leaders, law, and justice	**Social Classes**
The Arts	**Science/Achievements**	**Geography/Climate**
Religion importance of gods	**Moral Values** acceptable behavior	**Superstitions** magic, fate, beliefs

166

Create the "Greek Gazette"

Make a classroom magazine to reinforce the stories about Theseus. Bring in a variety of magazines as examples. As a class, determine what sections you would like to include in the magazine. (Some ideas have been included below.) Have students work in partners or individually to write and illustrate the different sections of the magazine. Combine them to form a book.

Suggested Magazine Sections:

Interviews—Theseus and any other character (remember to include an introduction and conclusion)

Self-Help—"Dear Ariadne" advice for couples in love

Health and Medicine—article by the Foot Washer

Home Decor/Home Improvements—article by the Stretcher and the architect of the labyrinth

Cooking/Recipes—article by Medea

Exercise—article by the Club Bearer

Business Section—Comparing business strategies by the two kings, Minos and Aegeus

Family/Child Raising—article by Theseus's mother, Aethea, and articles by the two kings

Travel—article describing the different places mentioned along with a map showing the routes

Pet Care—article about or by the Minotaur

Crossword Puzzle/Games

Theseus Dramas

Divide the class into small groups and have them create another obstacle for Theseus on the road to Athens. The problem should involve some kind of trickery rather than an animal-type monster. The scene should also teach Theseus an important lesson that he can use later in life. Have the students write, practice, and perform a brief drama about Theseus and the obstacle they have created. Evaluate each drama on its content. Did it show originality? Trickery? Did Theseus learn a lesson?

Letter to King Aegeus

Had Theseus sent a letter home to Athens before he set sail, his father would still be alive. Have students write a detailed account of Theseus' stay while on Crete. Have them describe his meeting with Ariadne, the exploration into the labyrinth, the battle with the Minotaur, and the fleeing of the island. Make sure students use a variety of figurative language to describe the places, creatures, and feelings of the characters. Choose a few examples to read aloud to the class and display.

Section 4—Orpheus

Comprehension Questions

1. In this version, the Underworld is referred to as Hades and the god is referred to as Pluto. Who is Hades? *(Hades is the Greek name for Pluto, the god of Death. If you wish, review the religion section pages 77–83, which describe the Greek belief in afterlife.)*

2. Why are people afraid to go to Hades? *(Accept reasonable answers.)*

3. Why was Orpheus able to enter Hades even though it was forbidden? *(His music was so powerful and magical that he was able to gain entrance even though he was mortal.)*

4. What does this story teach the reader about patience and curiosity? *(Accept reasonable answers.)*

5. Was Orpheus able to defy fate and bring back his wife from the dead? How is this consistent with the other myths that deal with fate? *(No, in the end he lost his wife because he didn't follow Pluto's instructions. This is the same as all other stories. When someone foretells the future, regardless of how hard the characters try, that future always comes true.)*

Comprehension Activities

1. Have students use the charts in their Literature Journals to record information about Orpheus, describing his adventures and character traits. Discuss as a class.

2. Have students locate examples of elements of Greek mythology in this story and record their findings in their journals. Discuss their conclusions as a class.

3. Have students draw a map of Hades on a large sheet of construction paper. Have them label each part and the path Orpheus took on his way to see Pluto.

Who Is More Powerful?

Have students review the description of Mount Olympus earlier in the book. How is Mount Olympus different than Hades? Remind students that Zeus and Pluto (Hades) are brothers, but Pluto was able to help Orpheus when Zeus was not. Debate as a class who is the more powerful god. As an alternative activity, have students write a persuasive compositions describing which god they feel is more powerful. Refer to pages 64-65 for directions for writing a persuasive composition.

Take My Advice

Have students write letters to Orpheus from a friend. In the letter, have the friend give his or her condolences as well as advice for Orpheus now that his wife is dead. What kind of modern-day messages would we send to help someone get over the grief of a loved one's death? How is this different than what Orpheus did?

Compare Myths

Have a group of students research to find the story of Proserpina (Persephone) and her kidnapping by Pluto (Hades). In this tale Pluto saw Proserpina and fell in love with her. He wanted to make her his wife, but she did not want to go with him. Proserpina was taken from her mother, Demeter, the goddess of the harvest. Demeter was so unhappy that she made the weather foul. Eventually, Pluto allowed his wife to visit her mother each year. While she was up on Earth the weather was beautiful. This particular myth explains why we have the different seasons.

Once students have found a few versions of the story, have them retell the story to the class through a drama. Have the class compare this trip to the Underworld with the journey of Orpheus. How are they similar? How are they different?

Superhuman You

Orpheus played magical music. Perseus could fly and become invisible. Hercules had superhuman strength. Have students imagine the gods have given them a superhuman quality for one day. What quality would they choose? What would they do with this new trait in one day?

Have your students write a description of their day with their new superhuman quality. Make sure they describe the quality, how they got it, the events of the day, their feelings, and a conclusion about what will happen once the day is over.

As an alternative exercise, have students present the information in a speech instead of a written composition.

Section 5—Meleager

Comprehension Questions

1. How is fate described in this story? *(Fate is three old women who spin at a wheel the thread of all mankind. They decide who shall live and who shall die.)*

2. How are the three Fates similar to the three Graeae sisters in the tale of Perseus? How are they different? *(They are all old women who are considered wise. Their conversations were overheard by the main characters, which caused some kind of action. They differ in that the Graeae sisters were witches with only one eye each. They did not control fate.)*

3. Was the mother able to defy fate after all? *(No, in the end Meleager died when the wood was burned up.)*

4. What does this story tell us about Greeks needing to praise the gods? *(The Greeks needed to thank all of the gods or they would be punished.)*

5. Based on the description of Atlanta, what characteristics are considered an asset for a Greek woman? Do these characteristics sound more like a woman of Athens or a woman of Sparta? Why? *(Beauty, grace, intelligence, musical talent, strength, speed, skill, and independence. These characteristics seem more applicable to a woman of Sparta since these women were athletic and allowed more freedoms than those in Athens.)*

6. Why did the skill of Atlanta anger the uncles? *(The men did not like to think that she had been brave when they had been afraid.)*

7. Do you think the mother was justified in putting the log back onto the fire? Why or why not? *(Accept reasonable answers.)*

8. Why do you think Meleager's mother soon died? *(Accept reasonable answers.)*

Comprehension Activities

1. Have students use the charts in their Literature Journals to record information about Meleager, describing his adventures and character traits. Discuss as a class.

2. Have students locate examples of elements of Greek mythology in this story and record their findings in their journals. Discuss their conclusions as a class.

3. Distribute sheets of construction paper. Have students list the main events of the story. Then have them turn this list into a cartoon strip illustrating and summarizing the main events of the story. Have students cut the paper into rectangles and connect them to make one long strip. Or they can draw all of the cartoon boxes on the one piece of paper like in the newspaper. Evaluate their cartoons and display a few examples in the classroom.

4. Have a group of students research what it might be like to go on a hunting trip back in Ancient Greece. Have them report back to the class about the weapons used, special clothing, strategies, etc. How accurate was the myth about Meleager in this regard?

Meleager Muses

In this story the author uses similes and personification to describe people, places, and events. Look at the examples from the story, then write your own examples of descriptive language using similes or personification as indicated for the items given.

Simile: Compares two things using the words LIKE or AS

Her hair was the color of gold, and <u>her skin was white as snow</u>.

The men flew from him <u>like leaves before the wind</u>.

Meleager battled <u>like a young lion</u>.

1. The three Fates_____

2. The wild boar_____

3. The trees in the forest _____

4. The arrival of Diana_____

Personification: Giving humanlike qualities to nonhuman objects

The <u>dancing light</u> of the fire <u>threw</u> shadows upon the wall.

The deep <u>rivers sang</u> as they <u>raced</u> on their way to the sea.

1. The night air during the feast in the woods

   _____

   _____

2. The arrow of Atlanta as it struck the boar

   _____

   _____

3. The sword of Meleager during the battle with his two uncles

   _____

   _____

4. The fire when the mother threw back in the log

   _____

   _____

Section 6—Jason and the Argonauts

Comprehension Questions

1. Why do you think Jason was raised by the Centaur? *(The Centaur was a great teacher. Accept other reasonable answers.)*

2. The story describes Jason's education in the woods. Which parts of his education sound like the education of Athenian boys, and which part sounds like the education of Spartan boys? *(Athenian—learning how to think, making poetry, and playing the lyre. Learning how to read and write. Spartan—sleeping on the hard ground and swimming in the cold river to make them brave and strong. Both Athens and Sparta—using the spear, sword, and bow; running; jumping; racing their horses.)*

3. Which heroes accompanied Jason on his voyage, according to this version of the story? *(Perseus, Hercules, Theseus, Admetus, Meleager, and Orpheus.)*

4. What two adventures are described on the way to the land of the Golden Fleece? *(They encountered birds made of bronze with feathers like arrows. They had to sail between two clashing islands without getting crushed.)*

5. Why do you think Medea helped Jason with the two labors dictated by her evil father? *(She said Jason was young and strong and she didn't want to see him killed. Accept other reasonable answers.)*

6. How did the king feel being tricked by his own daughter? What do you think he would have done to Medea had he caught her? *(Accept reasonable answers.)*

Comprehension Activities

1. Have students use the charts in their Literature Journals to record information about Jason, describing his adventures and character traits. Discuss as a class.

2. Have students locate examples of elements of Greek mythology in this story and record their findings in their journals. Discuss their conclusions as a class.

3. Draw a large Venn diagram and compare the Minotaur (Theseus' story) with the Centaur (Jason's story). How are they alike? How are they different?

4. Have students speculate on the life of Medea. At the time of the story she is young and willing to help Jason and his friends. Later, she tries to kill Theseus at the palace of King Aegeus, his father. Have students work in small groups to make a timeline of her life between the days of Jason and the days of Theseus. What happened to make her turn evil? Share ideas.

5. In each story the main hero is a male. Discuss with students why this seems to be the case in Greek mythology. What does this tell us about Greek culture? Are there any exceptions? *(Atlanta and stories about the goddess Athena show her strong and powerful like a man.)* Have students research other types of mythology and stories about heroes, including American tall tales. Are the majority of heroes male or female? Why? Do they think this might change over time? Why or why not?

Jason's Travel Log

Have students imagine that they were selected to join Jason on the Argo for his grand adventure. Have them write detailed travel logs describing the different events that happened on their journey using this page. Make sure they include descriptions of themselves as well as the other passengers. The travel log should express the feelings, hopes, and aspirations of the crew as they experience the adventure.

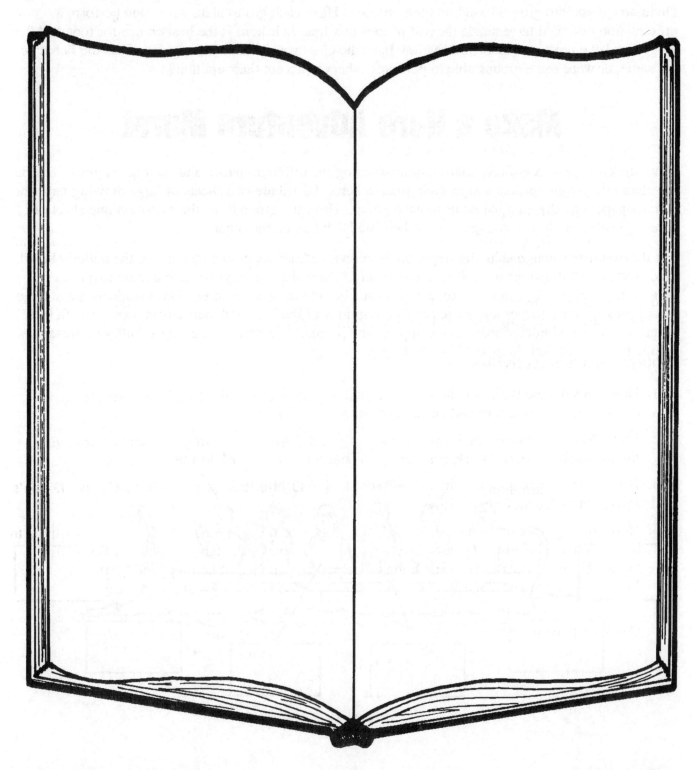

A Hero for Today

Now that they have learned about some heroes, have students evaluate the heroes' traits by writing an compositions. Tell students that they can choose one hero to have alive today. Which hero would they choose? What qualities does that hero possess that would make them valuable today?

As an alternative activity, have students choose the hero they would want to bring into the future. Divide the class into groups based on their choices. Have each group plan, write, and perform a presentation designed to persuade the rest of the class that their hero is the best choice for today. After all groups have presented their information, have the class vote on a hero for today. Was the outcome the same, or were some groups able to persuade others to accept their opinion?

Make a Hero Adventure Mural

Have students create a bulletin board mural depicting the different heroes and their adventures. Divide the class into six groups and assign each group a hero. Distribute two sheets of large drawing paper or butcher paper and drawing materials to each group. Have the group draw their hero on one sheet of paper. Have them draw a collage of their hero's adventures on the other sheet.

Cut the outline of a large ship, the Argo, out of brown butcher paper and attach it to the bulletin board. Place the cut-out drawings of each hero in the ship. Place the drawings depicting their adventures around the ship. Using colored yarn, connect each hero to their adventures. Have students make large nameplates for their heroes and write brief descriptions of the hero and their adventures. Attach these descriptions to the bulletin board in the appropriate places. Evaluate each group's ability to present a complete image of their hero and his adventures.

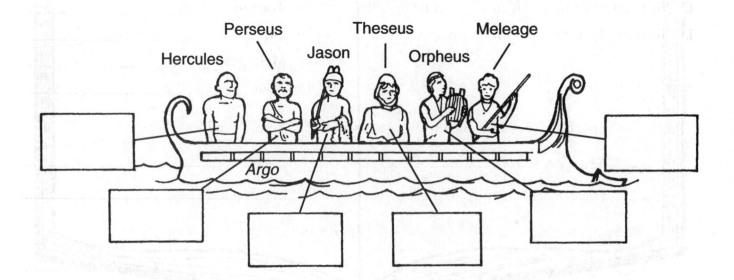

Literature Assessment

Match the hero to his description:

1. Hercules   A. Created magical music with his lyre.

2. Perseus   B. Had a huge boat built to find the Golden Fleece.

3. Theseus   C. Battled Death to save the life of another.

4. Orpheus   D. Was given a magic helmet and sandals from three witches.

5. Meleager   E. Killed a giant boar with the help of a woman.

6. Jason   F. Fought the Minotaur on Crete.

Give at least two examples from the book to describe each of these elements of Greek mythology:

7. Evil royalty _____

8. Son was not raised by father _____

9. Imaginative creatures with unusual capabilities _____

10. Use of magic _____

11. Influence of the gods _____

12. Belief in fate _____

Think about each myth. What were the main reasons each hero went on his adventure? Write the letter for each reason that applies to the myth. Some heroes may have more than one reason.

A. Went to help others in need of assistance.

B. Went to seek his rightful throne.

C. Was sent away by a king in hopes of being killed.

D. Went to gain something for himself.

13. Hercules _____

14. Perseus _____

15. Theseus _____

16. Orpheus _____

17. Meleager _____

18. Jason _____

19. In your opinion, which hero or heroes displayed the most heroic qualities? Why?

_____

_____

20. Name three things you learned about Greek culture from reading these stories.

_____

_____

Bibliography

Nonfiction

Burrell, Roy. *The Greeks*. Oxford University Press, 1990.

Cohen, Daniel. *Ancient Greece*. Doubleday, 1990.

Little, Emily. *The Trojan Horse*. Random House, 1988.

Loverance and Wood. *Ancient Greece*. Viking Press, 1992.

Miquel, Pierre. *Life in Ancient Greece*. Silver Burdett, 1985.

Nicholas, Robert. *Ancient Greece*. Scholastic, 1993.

Peach, Susan, and Anne Millard. *The Greeks*. Usborne, 1990.

Pearson, Anne. *What Do We Know About The Greeks?* Peter Bedrick Books, 1992.

Rutland, Jonathan. *See Inside an Ancient Greek Town*. Barnes and Noble, 1986.

Steel, Barry. *Greek Cities*. Bookwright Press, 1990.

Fiction

Connolly, Peter. *The Legend of Odysseus*. Oxford University Press, 1988.

D'Aulaire, Ingri and Edgar. *D'Aulaires' Book of Greek Myths*. Doubleday, 1962.

Evslin, Bernard, et al. *The Greek Gods*. Scholastic, 1966.

Fisher, Leonard. *The Olympians: Great Gods and Goddesses of Ancient Greece*. Holiday House, 1984.

Low, Alice. Greek Gods and Heroes. Macmillan, 1985.

McLean, Mollie, and Anne Wiseman. *Adventures of the Greek Heroes*. Houghton Mifflin, 1961.

Osborne, Mary Pope. *Favorite Greek Myths*. Scholastic, 1989.

Technology

Ancient Civilizations. Entrex. Learning Services (800) 877–3278. MAC/Win

Ancient Lands Microsoft 800-426-9400 Windows MPC or Mac

Chronology of World History. QUEUE. Learning Services (800) 877–3278. Win CD

Exploring Ancient Cities. QUEUE. Learning Services (800) 877–3278. MAC/Win/CD

Greek Art and Architecture. Video program. Alarion Press

Greece The Foundations for Greatness. Video program. Alarion Press.

History of the World. Learning Services (800) 877–3278. Mac/Win/CD

Mathology. Software. Lawrence Productions. 1–800–545–4677.

Where in the World is Carmen Sandiego? Learning Services (800) 877–3278. CD-Rom

Voyage Through the Magnificent Mediterranean. QUEUE. Learning Services (800) 877–3278. Mac CD/Win CD